ETERNITY

with your PETS

by

Caren Clevenger

Dedication

I dedicate this book to Catherine Clevenger, who taught me how to love and appreciate animals. Thank you Mom for making it possible for me to accomplish my purpose in life!

ALSO IN MEMORY~

In loving memory of Julie Bennett, who understood and recognized more than anyone the need for this message to go out. Thank you Julie — your prayers and encouragement helped me through some of my most difficult times of writing.

And for now, as you would always say whenever we parted — I say to you,

"I'll see you, at the appointed time…Ciao!"
…O Lord, You preserve man and beast

(PSALM 36:6 NKJV)

Contents

Preface

I DIDN'T WRITE THIS BOOK BECAUSE I LOVE ANIMALS.
I did the research because I do.

I DIDN'T WRITE THIS BOOK TO PROVE ANYTHING.
I have nothing to prove.

I DIDN'T WRITE THIS BOOK FOR MONETARY GAIN.
All proceeds go to the support of animal welfare—
and the advancement of the Kingdom of God!

I wasn't looking to write a book. In fact, the thought had never even crossed my mind until one day in 2002 when a friend emailed me something out of the blue. It was an article published by a major news outlet about how *Christianity is harmful to animals*. WHAT!? I thought to myself. As I read the article, I became painfully aware of the conflicting viewpoints between a well-known *animal rights activist* and a prominent leader in the Christian community. When I read what both had to say, I was grieved. Their argument concerned the sanctity of life. Regrettably, I disagreed with some of the Christian's comments, whereas I actually thought the animal rights activist had some valid points.

I wrote this book to resolve the fundamental differences between those two viewpoints, and the difference is: **all life is valuable and precious in the sight of God, but all life is not valuable and precious in the sight of man.**

The worst of it for me was when I realized this lack of understanding about animals has actually divided people and turned them away from a loving God!

The subject of *eternity* and animals seems to be a concern for a lot of people — *I know it has been for me.* Recently, I heard the pastor of a church make this statement, "I get four times more questions from people regarding *death*, heaven and their pets, than I do about their spouses." *Four times!?*

For as long as I can remember, animals have been a huge part of my life. I've had a multitude of dogs, cats, horses, a pet cow named *Thunder* and even a housebroken chicken named *Georgie*. My world has always included a vast assortment of animals, and life without them would be nearly impossible for me to imagine. Maybe you feel the same way.

As a major part of my life, animals have also been a part of my family. It is easy to trust them because they're honest and loyal. Hanging out with them provides a "safe place" — one of comfort, joy and peace. They don't hide behind masks, pretending to be something they're not; instead they're transparent, allowing us to see them for who they are — *no false pretenses.* Once you become friends with an animal, your friendship is for life. Their motive of love is genuine and always from the heart. But what is most amazing about animals is how they accept us for who we are — *shortcomings and all.*

As a young child I would sit sometimes for hours with my dogs, just looking at them in amazement — studying their markings and wondering if God Himself was the artist who selected and painted the creative artwork that was on each one. I was in awe of the unique patterns that appeared to be strategically designed by some supreme being. For example, my aunt had a horse named Honey with an image on her side that looked like a dog chasing a ball. *It was picture perfect* — as if an artist had used her for his own personal canvas.

Each individual design intrigued me — no two were the same. Likewise, their personalities were as different as their physical bodies.

Because I was in a position to interact with them on an intimate level, I was able to understand their thoughts, intents, and desires. Their instinctive ability and extraordinary *intelligence* amazed me. Quite often their intelligence went far beyond my own comprehension. *How did they get to be so smart*, I wondered?

I also noticed that their *perception* was far different from what I had observed in the actions of people. They seemed to operate on a level that appeared to be in a higher or different realm. It became obvious to me that animals were acutely more aware of what was going on in their environment.

But oh… the hardest thing I ever had to face was when one would die — oh such pain. My heart would break. In my desperation to understand why something as unnatural as the death of one of my pets could happen — *I was driven to seek truth.* To love them was right, and to lose them was wrong!

Over the years I have been with countless animals as they departed, and *never once did it ever seem right*. Did they just die and that's it — vanishing into thin air? Is that the end of them forever? *If not, where did they go?* Because of my great love and sincere passion for animals and their *welfare*, it was only natural for me to have a desire to know what their future held. *That is, if they even had a future.* And if they did — *I needed to know for sure if it included me.*

So, the purpose of this book is to reveal the truth that I've come to know concerning the *eternal destiny* of both man and animals.

I've spent many long years doing research to find this truth. It's a truth you want to know too and that's why you picked up this book. I pray that as you read these pages, you do so with an open heart, ready to see truth and experience that same love your pet already knows.

Now, it's time to answer the question for *mankind* once and for all — *Will You Spend Eternity with Your Pets?*

My Story

And when you leave,
What will I do?
How will I know,
I'll ever see you?

I believe that there are those of us who really, I mean *really*, love our pets in such a way that they've become part of our family, and not just simply some object of ownership. We love them in a similar way that a parent loves an *innocent* child who totally depends on them.

When we first come to know one another there is a supernatural bonding that happens, and then our love develops into a special relationship that touches the very core of who we are. With each bond there comes a permanent mark on our heart, always there to remind us of our endless love.

Many times I have wondered how it is that a species so different from my own is capable of freely giving and receiving the kind of love and affection I have often experienced.

Through my many years of being with animals, I have noticed that every one of them was able to connect and effectively communicate as though there were no language barriers. Even today, I find this to be amazing. And when I think about it, there is something significant and yet inexplicable about each and every one of them.

For a long time I was uncertain as to who or what was actually behind the orchestrating of such special relationships that connected me with a part of creation so different from myself. I was sure that anything as meaningful as these animals could not possibly have been a part of my life *by accident*. Even though it was a mystery as to how we came together, I was forever grateful to whomever or whatever was responsible for the impact they had on my life. *This awesome gift had to come from somewhere.*

And so, I'm writing this for those of you who share in my passion for animals and can relate to that very special relationship and deep love you feel for your pets. I *hope* this will help to answer for you, what has been my own greatest *need to know* in life — that foremost question: **when my pet passes, will I ever see them again?**

—————

Even though it was many years ago, my first experience is still so vivid in the eyes of my heart. It was the first day of November, on a cold, stormy Tuesday night — 7:30, and "Combat" was on TV — when a close neighbor frantically came to our door. "*Hurry*" Barbara screamed, "*There's been an accident, Babers has been hit by a car — they think she's dead.*"

In an instant, my parents were hysterically rushing out the door leaving me with my older brother, home alone. I desperately wanted to go and be with her, but mom insisted we stay.

All at once the sickest feeling I had ever experienced came over me. I thought, *can this really be happening?* It was worse than any nightmare.

I felt helpless — totally helpless. There had to be something I could do. I needed to do something, but what? It was all so sudden. As an eight-year-old child, I certainly was not prepared for this. My dog was *everything* to me, and my very best friend — *we were inseparable.*

Countless times, Babers had faithfully escorted me and my friend Phyllis to elementary school. Anticipating our routine departing spot, she would always remember to kiss me as we said goodbye — *every single day*. It was *there* at our place of departure that she knew to turn us both over to Mrs. Peel, our school's Safety Patrol Officer. Babers then longingly watched as we completed the rest of our short journey. It was a safe place for her, next to a fruit stand and away from the busy dangerous road.

I was always amazed by her loyalty, and how no matter what the weather conditions were, she patiently waited and watched the entire day for our return. Oh what dedication and responsibility it was for her to look after two young girls. Babers was a dog on an important mission, *and she understood her assignment.*

Babers and me

It wouldn't be until late in the afternoon that she would be able to spot us coming up over the hill. After crossing the road we were greeted by the smile on her face as she would collect us and then safely take me home from school. This was the way it went — *every day* — in the snow, the rain and the sun — Babers and I were inseparable. I belonged to her, and she was the *only* one that I was absolutely sure *really loved me.*

I began replaying over and over again that evening in my mind. She was with me only a few minutes ago. My Babers *always* went with us, Tuesday nights to the bookmobile.

Now I remember, she wasn't with us that horrible, nasty, rainy night for our trip home. I couldn't believe I left her behind. I had never done that before. Babers was street wise, and we didn't do leashes back

 Eternity with Your Pets

then. The traffic on Riggs Road was heavy at that time of night, and it was going from dusk to dark. Distracted by the downpour, Phyllis and I had made a quick dash for home, forgetting the most important one in my life — my dog, Babers. I was devastated. I thought, *What can I do?*

Then to make matters even worse, my older brother who was extremely upset and in somewhat of a state of shock, began to blame me. Unaware of my feelings and completely unprepared for the situation, he lashed out with words that cut like a knife. "*It's all your fault if she dies — you never should have left without her!*"

Now the guilt I felt on top of my pain, was overwhelming. *Oh my God, why is this happening?* All I could think about was — *I just can't lose her. Oh please, not now — not ever!*

While I was waiting, I didn't know how to pray or even who to pray to. *Was anyone even listening?* My heart knew there was somebody out there — somewhere, but I just didn't know how to make the connection. Time seemed like it would never end — an eternity, waiting for my parents to come home, and crying more tears than I felt could ever be possible. I was a wreck!

Babers was the one who always comforted me and now I was alone, left with this sick feeling deep inside my gut. *We were separated, but for how long,* I couldn't help but wonder. *Would they be able to bring her back to me?* For a moment I thought: *Yes, they need to hurry and bring her back, and make it right again. Please hurry! Does anyone understand? I just can't take the pain!*

Words could never describe the overwhelming feeling of helplessness that I experienced on that dark and gloomy rainy night — crying and waiting, and waiting and crying. *Babers please, just come home!*

Well, I wish I could say that's what happened — but it didn't. My parents had taken her to the vet clinic, but she *passed on* before arriving, never making her way back to me. I just went numb as I realized with that shocking fatal news — *that I never even had the chance to say goodbye.*

Burdened by my own feelings of pain and guilt, I could hardly relate to my family, but one thing I knew – Babers was not only an important part of life to each of us, but a very special and invaluable family member. Some outsiders may have called her a "mutt," (even though there was obviously German shepherd blood that ran through her veins), but I called her priceless because no amount of money could replace her. How do you put a price tag on endless, unconditional love? Babers was family and my very best friend.

I must have blocked out from my memory the rest of that night, because I really don't recall much after hearing the devastating news. It was all I could do to survive the pain and agony as it gripped every part of my being. A part of me was dead and the rest had nothing to live for. It was a torture, unlike anything I had ever experienced.

That very next day after the tragedy was a bright and sunny morning as we met for school, the same way we had every day since the first day of first grade. Except this time I was alone, without Babers. Phyllis had received the news that quickly spread throughout our neighborhood, and her heart was filled with love and compassion. She knew the loss. She felt my pain.

I thought, *how could last night be so dark and terrifying and just a few hours later the sun be shining so brightly?* But even though it was shiny and bright outside, my insides were numb and empty. I was heartbroken. I was just going through the motions, experiencing what it was like to have nothing to live for…

My everything was gone — seemingly to just disappear.

Now even many years later when I remember those moments, I can still feel the pain of separation. Even with time, those same feelings of love and pain have not changed. But there's a difference now, because I know some things I didn't know back then.

As a young child, I had many important questions, but there was no one with answers to give me the hope or comfort that I so desperately needed. Where is Babers? Where did she really go? Would I ever see her again? If I did, would she remember me?

All very logical and important questions for an eight-year-old whose life had suddenly been shattered by the tragic separation of her best friend.

I had a desperate need to know: *Will we be separated forever? Is this really the end for us?*

I wasn't interested in hearing what someone thought, or even what it was they might be wishing for. That wasn't good enough. How can something as important as the life and death of my best friend be such an *enigma* with so many unknowns? And why is it that the truth seemed to be hidden as though it was some sort of secret, with me only hoping that someday I would discover real answers to many heartbreaking questions? I needed someone to give me pure truth, and not some *"pie in the sky"* or make-believe *utopian* answer.

At the very core of my being, *I had the sense of knowing that there could only be one total and absolute truth.* And as much as I wanted to pick and decide Babers' **destiny** for myself, my heart knew someone much greater than me had already planned and prepared her future, long ago. So, what was the plan — the real plan, and not some fairytale Peter Pan version? In other words, *I don't want to be deceived, just give me the pure, unadulterated, Truth!*

I want those of you who might be suffering, or have already suffered the *passing* of your pet to know how very much I feel your pain, your sadness, and your sorrow. I have experienced that same unnatural separation many times and I know the deep level of cruel pain that it leaves behind. I also understand that if you don't already know the absolute truth, deep within there lies a strong desire not only for truth, but also for a *reunion* with the one you love and miss.

The good news is — *your pet does not have to be in your past.*

And when you leave,
What will I do?
How will I know,
I'll ever see you?

There is a Master Planner Who has laid out the *Perfect Eternal Plan*. The truth will become clear as we take a journey that will answer the many questions that have burdened and captivated our hearts. The revealing of truth will lead us to the plan for *eternal life*.

Your pet does not have to be left behind in the memory of your past. They can become a reality in your future, but only if you follow *God's Perfect Eternal Plan!*

1

Amazing Attributes

Marvelous are Your works,
And that my soul knows very well.

(PSALM 139:14 NKJV)

Life without animals

What would the world be like, if there were no animals? No birds to wake us in the morning. No fish to swim the oceans. No wildlife to inhabit the wild. No horses to graze the countryside. No dogs or cats to greet us after a hard day's work.

What would it be like if suddenly every animal disappeared?

When that question was posed to a large number of people, *everyone* expressed some form of loss. They said it would make them sad, depressed, lonely and incomplete. Others said the world would be a dismal, barren, bleak and empty place. A few couldn't even imagine a world without animals. Some thought their lives would be purposeless and others felt that *life without animals would be equivalent to living in hell.*

What about you? What would the world be like for you if suddenly there were no animals?

For me, a world without animals would be *desolate*. It would mean that the human race would never know one of God's greatest expressions of love.

I have discovered that the *characteristics* and *attributes* of animals are *significant and integral threads in the tapestry of eternity*. By design, they enable us to envision the Artist's perfected picture. Without animals, heaven's tapestry would be incomplete and man's *position* on earth would be pointless.

It's no coincidence that animals coexist among man. They were intentionally and strategically positioned that way by *divine providence*. (See Genesis 2:18-20)

There is a reason why you feel connected to your pet and why you can't imagine life without them. *You're not supposed to.* And there is a reason why your pet desires to interact with you and be a part of your family. It's because God placed that desire in them.

When God designed creation, He intended that we live together in harmony, forever. For *some* people, those relationships will continue on throughout eternity. But for others, the *plan of God will be ignored altogether — resulting in eternal separation from God, their loved ones, and their pets.*

Instinct or supernatural insight?

History records countless times where animals have either rescued or helped man, with no prompting or direction from us. Sometimes even risking their own lives. What would motivate them to do such a thing? I've listed some heroic feats below that demonstrate the amazing *characteristics* and *attributes* of animals.

- A dog named Tang *saved* 92 stranded sailors.
- Willie the parrot saved a 2-year-old from choking to death by screaming for help and repeating over and over, "Mama baby."
- A horse protected his owner from being trampled to death by a raging bull.
- A farmer's goat kept him warm and fed him for 5 days when he was stranded —saving his life.
- A pig stopped traffic to attract help for a lady who was having a heart attack.
- A cat warned her family that there was a carbon monoxide leak — just in time to save their lives.
- Three lions surrounded and protected a 12-year-old girl from kidnappers in Africa.
- An elephant lifted an 8-year-old girl onto his back, then took the pounding of a tsunami wave and saved her life.
- A gorilla saved the life of a 3-year-old boy when he fell over the fence at an Illinois Zoo.
- A Labrador retriever saved a drowning woman and brought her back to shore.
- Dolphins frequently protect and save human lives.
- A Beluga whale saved a drowning diver.
- There are numerous accounts of dogs saving loved ones from house fires.

And let's not forget — *Balaam's donkey!* (See Numbers 22:22-33, and 2 Peter 2:16).

Not only do animals rescue humans but animals also rescue other animals.

Documented stories such as these certainly substantiate that there is more going on inside the heart and mind of an animal, than simply mere *instinct*.

**Is it possible, that animals respond to man
with a heart of compassion —
because there is an eternal connection?**

Gifted with supernatural insight!

"Medical Detection" dogs have the ability to *forewarn* their owners of serious physical conditions. Life threatening diseases such as diabetes, seizures, heart attacks, blood pressure problems and even cancer, can sometimes be avoided. These supernatural abilities come from God and they not only *benefit*, but frequently save human lives.

"Service" animals help the visually and hearing impaired by acting as a substitute for their eyes and ears. Animals provide unique help for a variety of other disabilities that give man the gift of freedom and independence.

"Therapy" dogs provide comfort and affection. They are credited with improving the general well-being of people in hospitals, prisons, retirement homes and mental health institutions.

And let's not forget the "Search and Rescue" dogs. These animals have extraordinary abilities that are invaluable for tracking and locating missing persons in emergency situations. With their help, many lives have been saved! *When was the last time any one of us found a missing child through our sense of smell?*

**A bloodhound's sense of smell is so accurate, it can be used
as evidence in a court of law**

Many people recognize how valuable dogs are and just how much they contribute to our daily lives, and not only dogs, but also other animals. Did you know that cats also have a supernatural gift and ability to detect diseases? For instance, when a cat detects an illness in someone they love, they will try to get as close to that person as possible and purr. Their purring vibrations within 20-140 Hz range have been found to be medically therapeutic for many illnesses — particularly the healing and strengthening of bones. In fact, a cat's purring has been scientifically *proven* to heal bones. Veterinarians agree that these vibrations are a "natural healing mechanism."

Man has finally discovered, that there is more to a cat's purr than mere contentment. So, what other amazing attributes do animals have that we are unaware of?

Animals are gifted with many amazing attributes that humans simply do not have

People who refer to animals as being insignificant or mindless are only revealing their own ignorance and ego. They're usually the ones who think of themselves as being superior to animals, but the fact of the matter is, they don't know the truth. They don't understand that man was given superiority over animals in rank only, and placed in that special position to provide for their protection and care.

This special position that was given to mankind has become twisted in some peoples' minds. Some even believe it is their "God given right" to demean and harm animals if they so desire. That is not the will of God!

Even though man has the ability to perform heart surgery, this does not negate the intelligence and importance of animals. The truth is, animals have a unique and special intelligence that far exceeds our natural realm of comprehension. The reality is, we are oblivious to the many gifts and talents that God has placed within each and every one of them.

Sometimes animals know better than we do

A personal example that illustrates my own ignorance is when I attempted to load my horse, *Trinity* Dancer, onto a trailer. Due to an eye injury, I had taken her to the University of Florida, in Gainesville, for an exam. When the exam was over and it was time to go home, I was surprised when she refused to go near the trailer — *let alone load*. Understand, that at that time Dancer was a seasoned traveler and had more road time than most horses. Loading was previously not an issue.

It was a blisteringly hot day and the ordeal was becoming increasingly taxing. Then from out of nowhere, two men carrying a whip approached Dancer from behind. I had no idea who they were and they never asked if I wanted their help. I recognized that they were horsemen and I believed their intentions were sincere, but it was obvious by their demeanor and the way they approached us that their way of doing things was totally contrary to mine. I knew my horse and I knew what they wanted to do would have led to a total disaster! If I would have allowed them to help, it would have hindered the loading process and caused a breakdown in my relationship with Dancer. *Her trust in me was on the line.*

I didn't have to think twice; my mind was set. I was not about to give anyone, especially a stranger, an opportunity to whip my girl — *coercing and forcing her to load.* I politely thanked them but insisted they leave.

I've had Dancer her entire life, and I have witnessed her honesty and extraordinary intelligence. I knew disobedience was not the problem. *So, what was?*

Once the men were gone, I remember thinking to myself, *will I ever get her on the trailer? We can't spend all night out here.*

I decided to take her for a walk away from the trailer, and when I did, I calmed down and said, "God, You gotta help me. This is not Dancer. Something's not right."

When I became quiet inside I heard the Lord say in my *spirit,* "*It's the medication.*" In the next nanosecond I thought, *the medication? But, she's not staggering. Is it possible that's the problem?* Then I clearly heard the Lord say, "*She's got more sense than you do. She'll know when it's safe to get on.*"

So I motioned to Kenny (our driver), and explained to him that we would have to wait because the medication had been the reason she had refused to load. It wasn't long, maybe 15 minutes later, when *Dancer* decided to head back to the trailer. The medication had worn off enough to satisfy her and she promptly loaded with her usual confidence.

I realized then, if I had violated her good judgment by going against her will and allowing her to be manhandled, I could have placed her life in jeopardy. Dancer knew she lacked the necessary balance to take a safe road trip and I was delighted that she had taken a stand.

A few days later when we returned for the next exam, I informed Dr. Brooks about how the medication had affected her loading. I was thrilled when he agreed not to medicate her and consequently she loaded perfectly. *I had missed what my horse knew all along, and God was right — Dancer had more sense.*

Animals are in communion with God

There are many areas in life where animals excel far beyond our human capabilities. The problem is, we are blinded by our limited *knowledge* and preconceived ideas.

For example, we have concluded that birds migrate thousands of miles because they're preprogrammed by instinct. That is, we think they give no thought and have no choice in the matter. The reality is, if we were able to comprehend the magnitude of their intelligence, we would be astounded. If we ever recognized their *divine* connection, we would be in awe.

Why do we ignore what God said about the lights in the heavens? Didn't He tell us that the lights in the firmament would be for signs (signals) and seasons? (See Genesis 1:14) Yet we know very little about them and consequently we disregard God's instructions. (See Luke 21:11, 25 NKJV)

It's obvious to me that the animals are in relationship with God since they not only listen to what He says, but they also follow His instructions. Birds are a perfect example of how animals stay in tune with God and navigate by His divine direction.

Animals have creative intelligence

Not that long ago, man believed we were the only intelligent species because we created and used tools. This misconception was proven false when we discovered that chimpanzees, crows, dolphins and gorillas, just to name a few, also have creative abilities. If the truth were known, all animals have the ability to be creative, we simply lack the perception to understand their ways.

**When the time comes and the truth is fully revealed,
I believe that we will finally recognize that animals
have divine insight and abilities that far exceed our
finite knowledge.**

**When it's all said and done and the veil is lifted,
We will see that animals are connected to God
in ways we could never have imagined!**

Animals are an essential part of Heaven's tapestry. They are a vital and integral part of God's overall *perfect eternal plan!*

ALL THINGS WERE CREATED BY HIM AND FOR HIM
HE IS BEFORE ALL THINGS,
AND IN HIM ALL THINGS HOLD TOGETHER.

2

The Way

It is to Come!

The way it was in the beginning can never be fully understood by the human mind without the help of God. When man was first created and placed in the garden, everything he would ever need or desire was there and God Himself *saw that it was very good.* (See Genesis 1:31)

Love, joy, peace and happiness abounded everywhere. Nothing was lacking and nothing was missing. Man had it all! It was quite unlike anything we have ever experienced in this world today.

Man was in right relationship with God and the animals were his companions. Food was pure and abundant. The weather was ideal. Disasters were unknown and life was perfect in every way. There was no sickness, pain, strife or *death*. *The way it was* goes well beyond our limited imaginations. So, obviously something has radically changed from then until today.

The way it is today — is total *chaos*! Anyone existing on this planet in the Twenty-first Century can look around and witness not only starvation, but mass destruction and decay that continues to increase — invading and bombarding us all. *Evil* is escalating moment by moment, and unless you've become numb and totally desensitized, you can see that it's infiltrating everything! Some evil, is even too horrific to imagine.

Caught up in the midst of man's self-induced chaos are the innocent animals, along with the rest of creation. Without words to speak, their lives are at the mercy of man and they are subjected to "the **bondage of corruption**." (See Romans 8:21)

The animals have become victims and forced to live life in a fallen world in the midst of evil conditions that they themselves have no control over.

In spite of man's abilities, programs, politics and innovative technology, our world continues to deteriorate. The "*world system*" is rapidly declining, while the human race steadily plummets on a pathway towards imminent self-destruction! In man's vain attempt to be in total control, he's out of control, yet he continues on aspiring to make some sort of sense out of his *nonsense*.

Did God intend for our lives and the lives of the animals to journey on this downward spiral through the midst of chaos and ruin — *with seemingly no hope for peace and joy?*

What will be man's final destination? Will there be a happy ending?

We are all traveling through a given space on earth for an appointed time in history. Our very own heartbeat is keeping track of time — *time that will one day run out.* Then instantaneously, each one of us will *cross* over into a timeless realm *forever.* When this happens, whether we are prepared or not, we will have already made our choice — *one of **glory** or one of desolation.* Both are vastly different, yet permanent and real.

Deep in our innermost being we all know that there is much more to this life than what meets the eye!

Each one of us has made our grand entrance into this world by way of a mother. Most of us will go to school, some will get married and have kids, some will go to work, some will hope they make it to retirement, some will even grow old and yet *absolutely all will die* — and in between, there's a whole lot of *"stuff."*

Is that all there is to life? A meaningless short term journey here on planet Earth filled with *stuff* and then **THE END**? Are we like actors living out a part in a Hollywood script that eventually ends, only to be forgotten in a few moments?

It's sad to live without discovering what life is really all about — *idly passing through time with no purpose.*

An even worse case scenario would be to finally know that you had been tricked and deceived by lies, only to find out too late that you had missed out on the Truth of life.

How tragic would it be to discover in that instant, when your life abruptly comes to an end, that you have suddenly stepped into another realm; a realm you never knew existed?

You instantly find yourself in a place you never planned to be — *there's no way back and no second chance!*

The Bible tells us that this life, as we know it, is but a *vapor*, and as far as we can see, it's on an unstoppable progression headed towards *physical death*. (See Psalm 39:5, James 4:14)

When our time comes and we fulfill that imminent experience, will it result in one of mere non-existence, or will we be stepping into a forever unchangeable, eternal plan?

The answer to this profound question is not hidden *from* the hearts of people as some might suppose, but in actual fact, eternity has already been put into the hearts of each one of us. (See Ecclesiastes 3:11 NKJV)

Innately and instinctively every person knows there is an eternity and that one day they will face an almighty God.

At the very core of who we are, there is a knowing that an eternal existence is waiting for us *somewhere*.

We were all created to exist throughout eternity, and we are all powerless to terminate the *eternal* or endless time granted to each of us. *Physical death* is only a transition to a permanent crossing over. A birth date is only a record of when we entered time, as a death date will record our exit out of time. It is not the end *to us or for us — nor is it the end for our pets!*

Even though our timeline is unknown, we as human beings each have the power to decide where destiny will ultimately take us when our "deadline" arrives. We do this through one very important decision. A decision that is not only a privilege, but also a precious gift from our *Creator*.

Your pet's passing is different

Because animals were placed under man's *authority* from the beginning, they are not responsible for the *sin* that is in this world. They will never be held accountable for its consequences or required to pay its debt. Animals never rebelled against God. Unlike man's future, their future is secure and exempt from having to make a decision for *salvation*.

It is sin that causes separation from God. Animals themselves have never sinned; therefore, they have never been separated from God. Even so, they are required to live under the effects of sin in a *mortal body* made from a cursed earth that will one day die. They themselves have never done anything that would cause them to be disconnected from God.

Man's sin separates man from God.
Man's sin does not separate the animals from God!

The way it is to come —

God is the only One who *transcends* time and space; therefore, He knows *the way it is to come.*

God was 'there' even *before* the beginning of time because He resides outside of time. Remember, He is omnipresent and exists way out in front of us all in a timeless realm. God is not bound by the laws of this universe. This may be difficult to comprehend, but when you're in 'today' — *God was already there before you.*

Nothing ever has and nothing ever will slip past His omniscience. He is the One and only Creator of the entire universe.

God alone is *omnipotent* and holds the power to set the rules and call the shots — *always has and always will.*

God saw the 'Fall' even before it happened and had designed the *Perfect Eternal Plan* that would *overcome* any and all interference. He set the plan into motion even before there was a foundation to the earth. (See Ephesians 1:4)

God not only knows the future, but God holds the future because *God is the future!* He tells us in **His word** that if we choose Him, *the way it is to come* will be even better than *the way it was and the way it is.*

GOD'S PERFECT ETERNAL PLAN IS JESUS CHRIST
The One Who was, Who is, and Who is to come!

"I am the Alpha and the Omega, the Beginning and the End," says the Lord, "who is and who was and who is to come, the Almighty."

(Revelation 1:8 NKJV)

3

God's Perfect Eternal Plan

"Behold, I make all things new"

(REVELATION 21:5)

Everything created has purpose — everything created has destiny.

Nothing that exists *just happened*. This is true for man as well as the entire animal kingdom.

It's no accident that we are here together with the animals. Our coexistence is in the plan of God. We didn't just stumble into being, finding ourselves sharing the planet with a vast number of other *creatures* all by some *remote coincidence.*

Even though some might accept and believe in such an absurdity, the reality of *random chance* is virtually impossible. There is nothing random or accidental about *you* or *your pet's* arrival and timing here on planet Earth. Don't be fooled into believing some crazy notion that this *colossal* and complex creation came about by mere *chance,* or that it just *evolved* into its present condition. There is far too much evidence both scientifically as well as biblically that proves, "*In the beginning God created…*" (See Genesis 1:1)

**There is more to you and your pet—
than what meets the natural eye!**

Would the perfect plan be perfect without the animals?

God did not create man or animals simply for them to face a future of an unwanted death sentence! In His infinite love and wisdom, He designed a plan that would overcome an event that *no creature on earth could escape — called death.* (See Hebrews 9:27)

Contrary to what some believe, God's plan of restoration includes the animals, as well as mankind. Past patterns and events in the Bible prove this to be true. Whenever God made a provision or a *covenant* with His people, He also made a provision and covenant with their animals. (See the chapter, "What the Bible Says about Animals.")

His plan is infallible and absolutely vital for the rescue of *all creation.*

As I studied the Bible on the subject of *animals and eternity,* I was surprised to find that there are a large number of ministers who proclaim a message that contradicts what the Bible says. The essence of what they teach has led many to believe that God views animals as insignificant and completely unworthy of redemption.

What I heard them say not only grieved my heart but it also raised the following questions:

- Where in the Bible does it say that death is the end for an animal?
- Why would God have an eternal plan for man and not for the animals?
- If it is true that *God's plan of redemption* excludes the animals, then why did He put us together in the first place?
- If God simply *annihilates* animals at death, then why did He put such great love in our hearts for them?
- If the animals have no real value or eternal purpose to God, then why did He assign so many important and significant roles to them?
- And why would God include the animals in an *everlasting covenant* if they were not everlasting?

"The rainbow will appear in the cloud,
and I will see it and remember the *everlasting covenant*
between God and *every living creature of all flesh that is on the earth.*"
(Genesis 9:16 MEV)

As I already stated, many ministers leave people with the lasting impression that God is not concerned about their pets. This can be devastating, especially for someone who might be grieving over the loss or death of their pet. For some, it may have been their pets who loved and cared for them the most.

Isn't it vain to think that the eternal plan of God is all about man and nothing else?

The Bible certainly says otherwise. It clearly states that animals *are* included in God's plan of redemption.

The Apostle Paul tells us,

...creation itself also will be delivered
from the bondage of corruption
into the glorious liberty of the ***children of God***.
(Romans 8:21 NKJV)

If people are misled concerning the fate of their pets, it can easily result in their being turned away from God. But when we tell them the *good news* of the *Gospel* of Jesus Christ, they learn how He *redeemed all that was lost in the fall — including the animals*. With an understanding of truth, they will be drawn to God and not from God.

GOD'S ORIGINAL INTENT IS HIS FINAL DECISION

It was God the Creator who put mankind and animals together from the very beginning. We were put here for a reason and our relationships were intended to *glorify* Him. These relationships came straight from the heart of God and He never planned for them to terminate or cease to be. God's desire is for man and animals to live together — *for all eternity.*

God's plan was interrupted by the *fall of man*. Sin caused the *fall* and the end result was death. But even so — *the fall of man did not change the mind of God concerning His original plan for both man and the animals!*

That being said, there is still a great deal of confusion and controversy concerning what happens to both man and animals after death. Much of the contention that pertains to the animals has come from a misunderstanding of the following portion of *scripture*:

Then God said,

> "Let us make man in Our *image,*
> according to Our *likeness*;
> let them have ***dominion*** over the fish of the sea,
> over the birds of the air, and over the cattle,
> over all the earth and over every creeping thing
> that creeps on the earth."
> (Genesis 1:26 NKJV)

What does it mean to be made in the image of God?

When God made man, man was fashioned and designed to have a different role than the animals. Man was the only part of creation who was made in the *image* or *likeness* of God, and therefore the only one assigned dominion over the other parts of creation.

The meanings of these three important words, *image, likeness* and *dominion* are often misinterpreted. Knowing their original meaning is necessary in order to have an understanding of what was intended for the *man-to-animal relationship.*

It was with purpose that God chose to make man in His *image,* according to His *likeness.* The problem lies in that modern day vernacular often misuses these words as they pertain to this verse. In doing so, we miss the original intent of God.

The word *image* is described in the 1828 version of *Webster's Dictionary* as "a representation or similitude of any person or thing." *Strong's Concordance* says it is a "representative *figure."*

To be made in the "image" of God means: *man was intended to be God's representative here on earth.*

A representative is someone who bears the *character* or *power* of another, and a representative is an advocate who represents someone else's policy or purpose. Therefore, to be made in the *image* of God would indicate that man was to represent God on the earth and reflect what God Himself stands for.

It means that man was to have complete dominion or authority over the rest of creation, *indeed, over the entire earth.*

A misunderstanding of Genesis 1:26 may lead us to believe that animals are not *eternal spirit beings.* Many times I have heard fallacious comments such as, "Only man was made in the image of God, and God is a spirit. Man is different from the animals because he is a spirit being, and *animals don't have a spirit!"*

While it is true that man is a spirit, that is not the point to what is being said in the above passage. Angels are also eternal spirit beings but they are not made in the image of God either. (See Psalm 104:4)

So, to draw the conclusion that animals are not spirit beings based on what was said in Genesis 1:26 — is totally erroneous.

Also, it should be obvious that the subject of image is *not* referring to similarities of man's physical body as compared to that of God's physical body because God does not have a physical body.

Nor is it referring to the *soul* of man — his *mind, will and emotions.*

So, what does the word *image* in Genesis 1:26 refer to?
Answer: *Image refers to function!*

IMPORTANT POINT: In addition to a misunderstanding of the words *image* and *likeness,* many people don't realize that this passage was written using *Hebrew parallelism.* That means the two words *image* and *likeness* are actually synonymous and used interchangeably.

In other words, the *image* (Hebrew word tselem) of God is not referring to something different than the *likeness* (Hebrew word demuth) of God — **but rather *likeness* is used to emphasize *image.***

By using these two words together in the same sentence, they complement one another and add strength to the point that's being made.

To be made in God's image, according to His likeness, *was for the express purpose of exercising dominion!*

God's purpose in making man in His image was to represent His *dominion* and *authority* here on planet Earth. This was to be done in God's manner or way by following God's methods. That means man was created to *resemble* or *imitate* God in His nature and qualities.

The manner in which man represents God is by taking *dominion* the way God does. Man was made to reflect His Creator's nature and character and was subsequently given the position of *authority* and *dominion* over the Earth *and its creatures.*

IMPORTANT NOTE: When God made man in His image, *it was not to take away or diminish the value of animals,* but rather it was a way to describe the manner in which man ought to conduct himself. It was intended that man reflect the true *nature* and *character* of God. *Man was made in the image and likeness of God in order to fulfill his intended*

purpose. The outcome of his position was to ultimately be for the *benefit of the animals*, as well as all of creation.

Dominion may not mean what you think it means

What did God have in mind when He gave man *dominion* and *authority*?

It's important to know the answer in order to understand and appreciate how the man-to-animal relationship was meant to function.

> So God created man in His own image; in the image
> of God He created him; male and female He created
> them. Then God blessed them, and God said to them,
> "Be fruitful and multiply; fill the earth and subdue it;
> have **dominion** over the fish of the sea, over the birds
> of the air, and over every living thing that moves on
> the earth." (Genesis 1:27-28 NKJV)

God gave man two gifts to govern with from the beginning — *dominion* and *authority. Man was created to have dominion!*

Understanding the meaning of the words *dominion, rule* and *subdue* from a modern day, western culture viewpoint is quite different from God's original intent. Any animal lover who does not have an understanding of the original interpretation, would be troubled by the use of the words **dominion, rule** and **subdue** in the Scriptures — *I know I was.*

The way dominion is perceived in our society today — may not benefit the one placed under dominion

Dominion frequently carries with it the connotation that those under dominion are slaves and the one with the power of dominion is free to do whatever they want. NOT SO!

Dominion was not given for some *egotistical* power play, but rather as a responsibility to *serve* the ones you have dominion over. **God's idea of dominion was never an entitlement for** *exploitation* **or abuse, but rather a responsibility to care for and protect.**

So, what does it mean to have dominion God's way, and would this be good or bad for the animals who are under dominion?

If we go back to the origin of the words *dominion, rule,* and *subdue* and place them in the proper context and intent of biblical principles and concepts, they will convey a far different message than what some opinions suggest today. We must have a "kingdom mindset" which means we think about things according to God's established system.

Dominion is a type of authority that represents **WELFARE** towards its recipients and is demonstrated by the demeanor and conduct of the king himself. *The purpose for this authority is for blessing and not for harm.*

A righteous king or any ruler, when exercising true dominion is caring, loving, responsible and *benevolent.*

It is the personal responsibility of a king to operate in a manner that is for the good of his domain at all times and in accordance with God's nature and character. Welfare exercised the way God intended is beautiful and highly desirable by all, *including the animals.* It operates from love and will never bring fear or cause harm; instead, it always protects those under the dominion of the king.

Dominion is for the welfare of animals — Not their detriment!

Adam was the first man to be given a "kingdom" on earth along with *dominion* and *authority.* With that came a responsibility to the animals as well as the rest of creation. His position required that he actually "seek" out their safety and wellbeing at all times. By God's design, *animals were positioned to be totally dependent on man for their protection and prosperity.* When God gave man *dominion,* He was not trying to diminish the value of animals or any other part of His creation. It is essential for us to recognize that animals are a precious gift from the Lord and not to be taken lightly.

Authority was put in place for their protection, not their abuse!

God put man on the earth and placed him in a position of *authority* over the animals, as well as the rest of creation. He was given a kingdom that reflected God's kingdom in heaven, and divine order was set in place when

God said, "Let Us make man in Our image, according to Our likeness; let them have *dominion* over the fish of the sea…" (Genesis 1:26 NKJV)

The word *dominion* translates to *authority*, and authority represents responsibility with accountability. In the scope of things, *this is a major factor!*

When man was given authority it was never intended to be used to control, enslave or destroy, but rather to look after, protect and take care of.

When God gave man authority, it meant He placed man in charge. To be in charge makes you responsible. What was man responsible for? Answer: *Everything within his kingdom!*

If we do things God's way, then all of creation will benefit — including the animals. That's the way God's Kingdom operates, with order and structure. It's a Kingdom mentality!

SUBDUE — *the <u>earth</u>, not the animals!*
"…fill the Earth and subdue it;" (Genesis 1:28 NKJV)

Most people believe that subdue and rule (or dominion) have the same meaning, but they don't. There is a huge difference between the two.

Note: It was the Earth that Adam was told to *subdue* and not the animals. Remember, animals were originally presented to man as companions. *Subdue* is something you do to an *enemy*, not to a companion.

Man was instructed to have dominion over the animals and told to *subdue the earth*. Subduing included conquering, subjugating and bringing into subjection any and all enemies that might come and threaten the kingdom. If man were to subdue in concordance with God, subduing would provide for the *protection of the animals.*

It was vital for God to give man the instruction to *subdue* the Earth because of the satanic force he would soon be facing. Again, man's directive was to subdue the *enemy — not the animals.*

Man's charge was to subdue the earth for the animals' protection — It was never intended to cause them harm

In Genesis 2:15, "…the Lord God took the man and put him in the garden of Eden to tend and *keep* it." **KEEP** means to "guard and protect."

The garden was a place where Adam lived among the rest of creation. By means of the instruction Adam was given, he was warned that there would be something to guard against.

In summary: Man was given dominion and authority over the earth and put in the garden of Eden as God's *representative.* In that position, he was expected to *guard* and *protect* God's creation from an enemy named *Satan.* Therefore, Adam was responsible for the protection and welfare of God's entire creation. (See Genesis 1:27-28, 2:15)

THE FALL OF MAN CANNOT STOP THE PLAN OF GOD

All was perfect in the garden until Adam, by a single act of **high treason**, went against God and brought about an *interruption* to the master plan. His rebellion caused what is commonly referred to as the *fall of man.* This single act of rebellion changed *everything.*

In an instant, man lost dominion and authority over his entire kingdom. Consequently, *the whole creation went down with man in his fall.* This kept not only Adam, but also all of mankind for future generations, from coming to the source of life — God.

Prior to this catastrophic event, death was something that had never been experienced by man, or by animal. The *entire creation* had been designed to live *forever.* But now, man's fall brought death into the picture.

Death is the consequence of sin, sin against God

Before there ever was a fall, Adam fellowshipped with God in the garden. But after the fall, the life that Adam had previously known no longer existed. Now as a result of sin, man's spirit was cut off from God for all generations to come. Creation would have to suffer in a fallen condition, and the entire earth was brought under a *curse.*

As a result of the sin nature that entered the heart of the first man, sin is passed on in the hearts of his entire lineage from the moment they are conceived. This includes the *entire* human race, regardless of nationality. Man was incapable of helping himself. Only God could devise a plan that would provide for the redemption of His creation.

It is important to know that sin came on this earth through a man, not an animal. The animals have always been innocent bystanders, and consequently do not have any sin to pass on to their descendants.

Sin is not passed through the bloodline of animals!

As stated above, the sin nature of man passes on to each and every one of us through our father's bloodline, *whether we like it or not.* Romans 5:19 tells us that because of one man's sin, we were **MADE** sinners — *we did not have a choice.* As we all come to this earth, it is through our father's bloodline that we inherit our sin nature. We have no choice in the matter and *we cannot help ourselves.*

The seed of every man is now tainted and as a result, what man once ruled over now rules over him

Even worse than losing dominion over the kingdom that Adam had been given, was the fact that his sin had caused mankind to be separated from God. As a result, each and every one of us, no matter what sex, color, ethnic background, rich or poor, royalty or not, is born in sin. According to Psalm 51:5, we don't develop a sin nature *after* birth, *we are born with a sin nature.*

Historically, there has been only one exception to this pattern. This took place when God sent His Son to be born without an earthly *natural* father, through a virgin girl named Mary. Consequently, there was no contamination from sin in His blood — *it was an immaculate conception!*

God knew it would be necessary to send His own son Jesus into the human race to save all of mankind from the consequences of Adam's sin

— even before the foundation of the world. Romans 5:19 states, "For as by one man's disobedience many were *made sinners,* so also by one Man's obedience many will be *made righteous."*

There was only one way for God to circumvent the path of destruction that man had set himself on through his own disobedience and sin. Jesus was and is, the only sinless Man to have ever lived, thereby making Him the only one qualified to *redeem* mankind.

It was man's sin that *opened the door* which allowed a corrupt fallen angel, called Satan, to have a legal right to become the god of the "world system" — a system laced with every evil work that still wreaks chaos and havoc in our world today. This system not only affects and infects all of mankind, but it also hinders and causes harm to all of creation — *including the innocent animals.*

Without recourse, our pets have no ability to control or stop the effects of sin. They are therefore subject to sin's impact and have involuntarily been thrown into a state of chaos. However, the Bible tells us that they *eagerly wait* for the day when they will be set free from the massive corruption of sin. (See Romans 8:21 NKJV)

God's will never changes!

God's eternal plan for animals and their relationship to man, has not changed and will never change, because God Himself does not change. Unlike man, the Lord is consistent in His nature. He said in the Book of Malachi, "For I am the Lord, I do not change;" (Malachi 3:6 NKJV)

Whatever God has willed *will* come to pass — *no matter what.* His Word cannot fail. Always remember: God keeps His word; He never lies; what He says is true; and, He watches over His word to perform it. (See Jeremiah 1:12)

So, we need to find out what He has already said regarding our pet's future, as well as our own.

God never breaks a covenant promise!

It might surprise a lot of people to learn that whenever God made a promise and a covenant with man, He also included the animals.

For example, God said to Noah in the ninth Chapter of Genesis:

"And as for Me, behold, I establish *My covenant*
with you and with your descendants after you,
and *with every living creature* that is with you:
the birds, the cattle, and every *beast* of the earth
with you, of all that go out of the ark,
every beast of the earth.

Thus I establish My covenant with you:
Never again shall all flesh be cut off by the
waters of the flood; never again shall there
be a flood to destroy the earth."

And God said: "This is the sign of the covenant
which I make between Me and you, *and every
living creature* that is with you, for perpetual generations:
I set My rainbow in the cloud, and it shall be
for the sign of the covenant between Me and the earth.

It shall be, when I bring a cloud over the earth,
that the rainbow shall be seen in the cloud;
and I will remember My covenant which is between Me
and you and *every living creature of all flesh*;
the waters shall never again become a flood to
destroy all flesh.

The rainbow shall be in the cloud, and I will look
on it to remember the everlasting covenant between
God and *every living creature of all flesh* that is on
the earth.

And God said to Noah, "This is the sign of the
covenant which I have established between Me and
all flesh that is on the earth." (Genesis 9:9-17 NKJV)

In verse 16, He called it *the everlasting covenant*. An *everlasting covenant* between God and *every living creature of all flesh that is on the earth.*"

Everlasting means it will never stop. It will last forever.

Why would God give a living creature an everlasting promise, if He didn't intend for that creature to live forever?

He wouldn't!

God is not slack about what He promises, and He does not make covenants halfheartedly. (See 2 Peter 3:9)

We must never confuse God's ways with man's ways.

Another important aspect concerning the making of a covenant is the relationship that God has with animals. We can observe in the story of the great flood that *God does communicate with animals.* And why not, He created them. (See Genesis 7:6-9)

If God can give directions to an animal, can He not make an agreement with them?

Would God make a covenant with a creature that couldn't understand? No, He wouldn't.

First of all, there would be no covenant without mutual understanding between the parties. Secondly, it would be disingenuous of God. Therefore, even though we may not fully understand how God communicates with the animals, *the Bible makes it clear that He does.*

IMPORTANT NOTE: Hosea 2:18 tells us that God *will also include the animals in His New Covenant.*

"In that day will I make a covenant for them
With the beasts of the field,
With the birds of the air,
And with the creeping things of the ground.
Bow and sword of battle I will shatter from the earth,
To make them lie down safely." (Hosea 2:18 NKJV)

Since God is Spirit, could He not communicate with His animals, Spirit to spirit?

THE PLAN OF GOD UNFOLDS!

Your kingdom come;
Your will be done on earth, as it is in heaven.
(Matthew 6:10 MEV)

There will come a time in the future, when the redeemed of the Lord will return to this very same earth, along with the animals. At that time, the earth will have been completely *restored*. It will no longer be in the same sinful, decaying condition that we experience today. Its restoration will even surpass the magnificent place that it once was back in the garden of Eden.

The earth will again be populated with not only our pets, but also an abundance of all types of animals. Jesus *Christ* will rule and reign, and those who are redeemed, along with the animals, will join together and live in a permanent state of peace and harmony — *the way it was before the fall of man.* (See Isaiah 11:6-9)

We can know that this will come to pass because God's original intent was to have a kingdom on earth that reflected His Kingdom in heaven. We can be sure that His plan will succeed not only because of who He is, but also because of His eternal *covenant promises*.

Ultimately, love will cover the entire earth and Peace will reign forever.

SATAN DIDN'T WIN!

If man's fall had resulted in the eternal loss of the animals, Satan would have gained a victory over God concerning that part of His creation.

But Satan never has and never will have victory over God in any area!

And having disarmed authorities and powers,
He made a show of them openly, triumphing over them by the cross.
(Colossians 2:15 MEV)

At the completion of creation, *God saw that everything He had made was very good.* (See Genesis 1:31) Therefore, if the animals were anything other than restored to their original condition, it would mean either God changed His mind or Satan triumphed.

However, we know that God's plan for man, the animals and the earth has *not changed* because God Himself declares,

"For I am the Lord, I do not change..." (Malachi 3:6 NKJV)

If the animals' destiny was one of hell or annihilation, would that be just? NO!

God is a just judge, and God is angry *with the wicked* every day.
(Psalm 7:11 NKJV)

There would be no justice if Satan won where any part of creation was concerned

We also know that Satan did not defeat God concerning the animals, because *Jesus destroyed the works of the devil!*

He who sins is of the devil,
for the devil has sinned from the beginning.
For this purpose the Son of God was manifested,
that He might destroy the works of the devil.
(1 John 3:8 NKJV)

GOD'S PERFECT ETERNAL PLAN IS REDEMPTION!

Again, the mess that this world is in was never the desire of God, but rather the consequence of man's rebellion. But in spite of man's sin, God still has the *perfect eternal plan* at work for a total restoration. It is a plan that not only saves mankind from *eternal death*, but also redeems the *animals from the consequences of man's sin.*

Animals were merely caught up in the cross fire of sin— They belong to God, not to Satan!

If we accept Jesus and what He did for us on the cross at Calvary, *we will be saved.* And through the shed blood of Jesus, the animals will also be restored to their rightful position and original condition. However, if we reject God's plan of salvation, there will be no hope of ever being reunited with God, our family, our friends, *or our pets.*

**For the redeemed or the saved,
the interruption caused by man's fall
is merely a temporary separation from their pets when
they pass**

It is through Jesus Christ, and Him alone that we can regain *all that was lost* through the disobedience of Adam. It was the *sacrifice* of God's own Son that solved the catastrophe caused by the fall. And it was His victory on the cross that brought *salvation to both man and animal!*

...man and beast you save, O Lord.
(Psalm 36:6 ESV)

Man's fall could not stop the eternal plan of God!

*Jesus will rule and reign forever with those
who love and accept Him!*

"The kingdoms of this world have become
the kingdoms of our Lord and of His Christ,
and He shall reign forever and ever!"
(Revelation 11:15 NKJV)

There will come a time when the earth will be cleansed by fire, and then restored to the condition that it was originally intended to have. This is referred to as the New Earth. (See 2 Peter 3:7, 10) The redeemed of the Lord will come back to the earth — *along with the animals,* and live the peaceful life that God planned for all His creation from the beginning.

Redemption in Jesus Christ means the restoration of God's original *good creation*. (See Acts 3:21)

Nevertheless we, according to His promise,
look for new heavens and a new earth in which righteousness dwells.
(2 Peter 3:13 NKJV)

DEATH DOES NOT TRANSLATE TO NON-EXISTENCE!

GOD'S PERFECT ETERNAL PLAN IS REDEMPTION

Free from Eternal Death

Therefore if the Son sets you free,
you shall be free indeed.

(JOHN 8:36 MEV)

Did you know that there are three kinds of death written about in the Bible?

The first kind of death is *spiritual death*. Spiritual death does not mean that the spirit ceases to exist, it's far more devastating than that.

The moment Adam committed *high treason* against God, by disobeying His command and eating from the forbidden *tree of the knowledge of good and evil*, it caused the fall of man. Spiritual death was the outcome of his rebellion. The result was catastrophic not only for Adam, but also for the entire human race.

Tragically, Adam's sin caused a spiritual separation to take place between mankind and God — *the source of all life.*

So, what is the cause of spiritual death?

Sin!

What is sin?

The original translation of the word 'sin' means "to miss the mark" of God's *holy* standard of *righteousness*. The *mark* is the standard of perfection established by God. To sin is to violate the revealed will of God.

All sins are an offense to God and *sin separates us from God.* (See Isaiah 59:2)

The first spiritual death

The first mention of death in the Bible is where God warned Adam that there would be a fatal consequence if he ate from the forbidden tree of the knowledge of good and evil.

> And the Lord God commanded the man, saying,
> "Of every tree of the garden you may freely eat,
> but of the tree of the knowledge of good and evil
> you shall not eat,
> *for in the day that you eat from it you will surely die.*"
> (Genesis 2:16-17 MEV)

The fatal consequence was *spiritual death.* The day that Adam ate the fruit, he died spiritually. This does not mean that Adam's spirit died because spirits don't die; *spirits are eternal*. What this means is, Adam's spirit was instantly disconnected from the source of life — *God*.

Spiritual death means that fellowship between man and God has been broken.

Spiritual Death separates man from God

But your iniquities have separated you from your God;
And your sins have hidden His face from you,
So that He will not hear. (Isaiah 59:2 NKJV)

As a result of Adam's fall, sin entered the world. Adam, the head of the human race, caused every man after him to be born into a sinful state.

Behold, I was brought forth in iniquity,
And in sin my mother conceived me.
(Psalm 51:5 NKJV)

No matter who we are, at the time of birth, *we are all born spiritually dead* because we all have inherited the sin nature from our father — Adam. We were created to be in the presence of God, but we are born spiritually separated from Him because of our sin nature. *There is only one exception — Jesus Christ!*

There is no spiritual death for the animals

Every human being is born *spiritually dead*, but this is *not true* for animals. Adam's sin did not bring spiritual death to the animals because they did not inherit his sin nature.

Adam's sin infected mankind — not the animals!

The bottom line is: *animals are not born dead in sin*. And because they are sinless, their relationship with God has never been broken. This means that animals are born *spiritually alive*. This is why animals do not need to be *born again* in order to spend eternity with God.

On the other hand, to be *born again* is the *only* way for man to be saved, and the *only* way for man to spend eternity with God and loved ones. (See John 3:3)

The sin of Adam did not affect
the spiritual relationship animals have with God

The second kind of death is *physical death* — this takes place when the spirit and the soul depart from the body. Physical death is obvious to us all because we can see and experience it with our eyes. It is tangible. And we know from the Bible that there is more to us than just a physical body; the Book of James tells us – *the body without the spirit is dead.* (See James 2:26)

When Adam ate from the tree of the knowledge of good and evil, his rebellious act not only brought sin into the world, but it also caused a curse to come upon the ground. There is a direct correlation between man's sin and the land. The earth is affected by sin and expresses itself with manifestations of earthquakes, hurricanes, tsunamis and volcanoes — just to name a few.

"*...cursed is the ground because of you...*" (See Genesis 3:17-19)

Why is this significant?

The curse that was put on the ground is important because it brought about the process of death and decay. Every material thing on the earth is derived from the ground and is subject to the effects of the curse and consequently will die and decay.

Think about it: what does the Bible tell us that the bodies of both man and animals are made from? The ground! (See Genesis 2:7, Ecclesiastes 3:20)

This is the reason why *all bodies* will die and decay.

Physical death
is the only death that animals will ever experience!

Even though the Bible talks about three deaths, there is only *one* death that animals will ever have to face — the death of their physical body.

This means that there will come a time in every animal's life when *their spirit will depart from their body and return back to God.*

> Then the dust will return to the earth as it was,
> And the spirit will return to God who gave it.
> (Ecclesiastes 12:7 NKJV)

Again, every man's body and every animal's body will one day die because they are made from the ground — *ground that is still under the curse.*

> (See Genesis 3:17-19)

IMPORTANT NOTE: *Even though every animal will experience physical death, there is coming a time when every animal will also experience the resurrection of their body.* (See Romans 8:20-23) (Also see "The Promise of the Resurrection" chapter)

The *third* kind of death is *eternal death* — the Bible calls this the **second death**. (This *second death* must not be confused with the second kind of death, referred to above as physical death.)

Eternal death is different from both *spiritual death* and *physical death* because *eternal death is everlasting.* It is an unending separation from God, our pets and everyone else — that is, *for all who have rejected Jesus Christ.*

Despite what some believe, *eternal death is not having an everlasting party with other sinners.* Eternal death is the ultimate form of separation!

When a spiritually dead person (someone who has not been born again) dies physically, they enter eternity separated from God — *this is called the second death.* Once someone enters the *second death, it is irreversible* and there is no future hope for them.

What the Bible calls the "second death" is eternal, *and in the **lake of fire!***

> But the cowardly, the unbelieving, the abominable, the murderers,
> the sexually immoral, the sorcerers, the idolaters, and all liars shall
> have their portion in the **lake which burns with fire and brimstone.**
> **This is the second death.**
> (Revelation 21:8 MEV)

However, the Good News is that if we overcome, we will not have to experience the second death.

> The one who overcomes will **not be hurt at all by the second death**.
> (SeeRevelation2:11)

So, what does it mean to overcome?

God has given all of mankind, *one way* to overcome the *second or eternal death*—and *the way* is through His Son, Jesus Christ.

> Jesus said to him, "I am **the way,** the truth, and the life.
> No one comes to the Father except through Me." (John 14:6 NKJV)

No one has to end up in a place of *eternal damnation*, except by their choice. Everyone who receives Jesus Christ as their personal **Lord and** *Savior* will be able to *overcome* and will be *saved from the eternal second death*.

When Jesus speaks of *he who overcomes* in Revelation, Chapters 2 and 3, He means those who are trusting in His blood for their salvation. In other words, *all born again believers* will be saved from the *second death!* It's having faith in Jesus Christ that makes you an overcomer!

> …for whoever is born of God overcomes the world,
> and the victory that overcomes the world is our faith.
> (1 John 5:4 MEV)

THE TRUTH ABOUT ETERNAL DEATH

There are those who may debate it, but the Bible clearly teaches the *doctrine* of *eternal death*. The following three passages leave no doubt:

> And many of those who *sleep* in the dust of the earth shall awake,
> Some to **everlasting life,**
> Some to shame and **everlasting contempt.** (Daniel 12:2 NKJV)

> And these [the wicked] will go away into **eternal punishment,**
> but the righteous into **eternal life.** (Matthew 25:46 ESV)

And if anyone's name was not found written in the **book of life,**
he was thrown into the **lake of fire.** (Revelation 20:15 ESV)

Revelation 20:10 tells us that the *Lake of Fire* burns *forever and ever.*

Again, there is good news; *no one has to end up in the lake of fire!* Jesus,
Himself gives us that assurance in John 6:37,

"…the one who comes to ME I will by no means cast out." (NKJV)

We have all been given the gift of eternal life, but it can only be received through Christ Jesus.

For the wages of sin is death, but the gift of God
is eternal life in Christ Jesus our Lord.
(Romans 6:23 NKJV)

For God so loved the world that He gave His **only begotten Son,**
that whoever believes in Him should not perish but
have *everlasting life.*
(John 3:16 NKJV)

"Most assuredly, I say to you, he who hears My word
and believes in Him who sent Me has *everlasting life,*
and shall not come into judgment, but has passed from death into life."
(John 5:24 NKJV)

"And these will go away into everlasting punishment,
but the righteous into *eternal life.*"
(Matthew 25:46 NKJV)

The choice is set before each one of us. If we decide to receive Jesus Christ
as our Savior, we will be saved and receive eternal life. But, if we reject the
Son of God and what He did for us on the cross at Calvary, *we condemn
ourselves to eternal damnation — in the Lake of Fire.*

"For by *your* words *you* will be *justified,*
And by *your* words *you* will be *condemned.*"
(Matthew 12:37 NKJV)

The Bible tells us,
that we are the ones who decide our eternal destiny

NO ONE CEASES TO EXIST!

It is imperative to understand that *death* in the Bible *always* refers to some form of separation. Despite what some believe, the *second death* is not referring to annihilation, non-existence or unconsciousness. The spirit of a man and the spirit of an animal — *will never die!*

Nowhere in Scripture does it ever say that man or animal ceases to exist.

No matter how hard man tries to stop the progress of mortality; *physical death* is inevitable. No one, including the animals, will be able to escape the *appointed time* when their spirit and soul *depart* from their body — *physical death.*

Death is not an accident — death is an appointment!

And as it is appointed for men to die once,
but after this the judgment…
(Hebrews 9:27 NKJV)

Notice that this verse tells us the *judgment* is an appointment for man; *and not the animals.*

Spiritual death and the *second death* are both vastly different from *physical death,* because they are separation from God. *Spiritual death,* is the *spiritual* condition into which every person is born. The reason we were born this way is because we all inherited the sin nature from our father — Adam.

Again, this is not the case for the animals. Animals are not born *spiritually dead* because they themselves are sinless. Spiritual death involves sin.

Unlike Adam's descendants, animals have not inherited a sin nature from their ancestors. The spirit of an animal has never been affected by man's fall, and therefore they are not spiritually separated from God.

You choose your eternal destiny!

Now, as far as the *second* or *eternal death* is concerned, each one of us still has a choice to make. When we recognize the fact that we are a sinner, and confess with our mouth that Jesus is Lord and believe in our heart that God *has* raised Him from the dead, the Bible says, *we will be saved.* To be saved means, to be *born again.*

> ...because, if you confess with your mouth that Jesus is Lord
> and believe in your heart that God raised him from the dead,
> *you will be saved.* For with the heart one believes and is justified,
> and with the mouth one confesses and is saved. (Romans 10:9-10 ESV)

When we do this, the *spiritually dead* condition that we were born into is instantly reversed. At that moment, we become what the Bible calls, *born again* — or spiritually alive. We have reconnected to the source of all life — God.

This born again experience is the greatest miracle of all!

To be *born again* is the *only way* for man to be brought back into a right relationship with God. And the only way to be *born again* is through the shed blood of Jesus Christ and by the power of the Holy Spirit.

The term *born again,* literally means 'born from above.' When someone is saved, that means they have been *born from above* or spiritually renewed, and consequently they have become a ***child of God***. (See John 3:3, and 2 Corinthians 5:17)

Jesus Himself proclaimed:

> "Most assuredly, I say to you, unless one is born of water
> and the Spirit, he cannot enter the kingdom of God." (John 3:5 NKJV)

Unless you are *born again,* you absolutely cannot go to heaven; and unless you are *born again,* you absolutely will never see your pets again!

The only way to escape eternal death is to be born again

Eternal death is not a matter in question for the animals

The reason the Bible doesn't talk about the *second death* for the animals is because they will *never* experience the *second death*. They will *never* experience the *second death* because they never experienced the first death — which is the death that every human being is *born into*.

And because the spirit of an animal never dies or separates from God to begin with, there is no need for their spirit to be reconnected — *born again*.

Consequently, animals will only have to face one death, and that death is *physical* — a *temporary* separation of their spirit and soul from their body.

What does it mean to be 'born again?'

The first mention of the term 'born again' is found when Nicodemus, a ruler of the Jews, came to Jesus *in the night* seeking the truth about God and eternal life.

"Rabbi, we know that You are a teacher come from God;
for no one can do these signs that You do unless God is with him."

Jesus answered and said to him, "Most assuredly, I say to you,
unless one is born again, he cannot see the kingdom of God."

Nicodemus said to Him, "How can a man be born when he is old?
Can he enter a second time into his mother's womb and be born?"

Jesus answered, "Most assuredly, I say to you, unless one
is born of water and the Spirit, he cannot enter the kingdom of God.
That which is born of the flesh is flesh,
and that which is born of the Spirit is spirit.
Do not marvel that I said to you, '*You must be born again*.'
The wind blows where it wishes, and you hear the sound of it,

but cannot tell where it comes from and where it goes.
So is everyone who is born of the Spirit." (John 3:2-8 NKJV)

In order to understand what it means to be *born again*, we need to know that the Bible talks about *two births*. The 'first' birth is the *physical birth* where each one of us comes into this world through the union of a woman and a man. This birth is referred to as being 'born of water.' This birth is NOT referring to baptism.

The 'second' birth is a *spiritual birth*. This means to be born of the Spirit — God, the Holy Spirit. When we are *spiritually born*, God's Holy Spirit "quickens" us or makes us alive.

So when the Bible speaks of being *born again*, it actually means to be born for the second time. We are all born the 'first' birth — the *physical birth*, but not all will choose to be reconnected to the Spirit of God through the *second birth* — which is the *born again* experience. And without the *second birth*, we will remain *spiritually dead*.

It's been said:

If you are born once, then you die twice.
If you are born twice, then you die once.

You know it when you're spiritually alive, but you don't know it when you're spiritually dead!

I tell you this because of my own experience. When I was *lost and spiritually dead*, I had no idea that this was my spiritual condition. If you had asked me then if I believed in God, I would not have hesitated to say, *yes*. It had always been obvious to me that there was a God just by looking at creation — *especially the animals*. But I never knew that I could actually *know* God.

If you had told me that I was *spiritually dead*, I would have been highly insulted. I considered myself to be a *spiritual person*. My friends even told me how spiritual I was. But little did I know that I was actually *spiritually dead*. I didn't understand my true spiritual condition until *after* I asked

God to forgive me of my sins and to come into my heart and be my Lord and Savior. The moment I did this, it was as though *scales* fell off of my eyes and my heart.

There was an immediate change that took place in me, and it was so radical that no one had to tell me I was *born again — I knew it!* As a matter of fact, I had never even heard the term *born again*, but somehow I knew that *I had been changed.*

Even colors were different. They were far more vibrant and intense, almost alive with a brilliance that I had never seen before. It was as though I was seeing the truth of what colors were meant to look like. I believe, I was seeing the colors of heaven.

From that moment on, there were many changes in me but the one that stands out the most is *love. Love from God — love for God —and love for other people.* This love is different from worldly love. It is a supernatural love, and it is a love that no one can experience or even understand unless they are *'born again from above.'*

This is because it's God's love, and no one can understand or experience God's love unless they are *spiritually reconnected* to God Himself.

You must be born again
in order to recognize that you were once spiritually dead!

The Bible tells us that Satan blinds the minds of unbelievers.

> …whose minds the god of this age has blinded,
> who do not believe, lest the light of the gospel of the glory of Christ,
> who is the image of God, should shine on them.
> (2 Corinthians 4:4 NKJV)

God wants to take the scales off of your eyes. He wants you to know the truth and to be filled with His Holy Spirit. We read about this in the book of Acts, where He removed the scales from Saul's eyes.

Immediately there fell from his eyes *something* like scales,
and he received his sight at once; (Acts 9:18 NKJV)

THE BOTTOM LINE IS —

All will experience — *including the animals*
Physical death

If you *accept* Jesus, you will only experience two deaths
Spiritual and physical

If you *reject* Jesus, you will experience all three deaths
*Spiritual, physical and **eternal***

*Three strikes and you will be **cast out**!!!*

But the good news is — you don't have to be cast out.

"All that the Father gives Me will come to Me,
and the one who comes to Me I will by no means **cast out.**"
(John 6:37 NKJV)

Note: There may be a question as to why those who have accepted Jesus Christ as their Savior would still experience spiritual death. Let me remind you, *everyone is born spiritually dead.* This means that every person has experienced spiritual death, whether they are *born again* or not.

[But, as for the animals — they will experience only one death — *physical.*]

A LOVING GOD, IS A JUST GOD!

Those who reject the idea of eternal damnation find it difficult to believe that a loving God would allow people to go to a place as horrific as hell *and for all of eternity.* They don't understand that even though God is a

God of love, He is also a God of justice, righteousness and holiness — and it was His love that provided *the way* to escape His wrath.

That way is through the sacrifice of God's only begotten Son, Jesus Christ.

> "For God so loved the world that He gave His only begotten Son,
> that whoever believes in Him should not perish
> but have everlasting life.
>
> For God did not send His Son into the world to condemn the world,
> but that the world through Him might be saved.
> He who believes in Him is not condemned;
> but he who does not believe is condemned already,
> because he has not believed in the name
> of the *only begotten Son* of God." (John 3:16-18 NKJV)

When a person is born, that person can never die. Every human spirit goes on forever and ever after this physical life in one of two places — either in heaven or in hell. *You choose your own destination!*

Animals, on the other hand, do not make a decision concerning heaven or hell. Their destiny is already secure with God along with every person who has accepted Jesus Christ as their personal Lord and Savior.

**Whether its spiritual death, physical death or eternal death,
death is the result of man's choice
— And not the will of God!**

- How many deaths does the Bible talk about?
  Answer: Three

- What are they?
  Answer: Spiritual, physical and eternal — *which is the second death*

- What does the word death mean in the Bible?

  Answer: Separation

- What is meant by physical death?

  Answer: Spirit and soul separating from a body

- What is meant by spiritual death?

  Answer: Spiritual death is when the spirit of man is separated from God

- Who has experienced spiritual death?

  Answer: Every human being ever born

- Who remains spiritually dead?

  Answer: Everyone who chooses not to be born again

- Who is spiritually alive?

  Answer: Every person who chooses to be *born again — and the animals*

- What happens to a spiritually dead person when he dies physically?

  Answer: He dies what the Bible calls the second death — *which is eternal*

- What is the second death?

  Answer: Man's eternal separation from God

- Who will experience the *second* (eternal) *death?*

  Answer: All who reject Jesus Christ as their personal Savior

- What is the one death that an animal will experience?

  Answer: Physical death

- What are the two kinds of death that animals will *never* experience?

  Answer: Spiritual death and eternal death

- Who is it that is *free from the second* (eternal) *death?*

  Answer: The people who are saved and *born again —*
  And the animals who don't need to be saved or born again!

- What is eternal life?

  Answer: Eternal life is more than living forever in heaven.
  Eternal life is knowing God through His Son, Jesus Christ.
  Eternal life begins the moment you are *born again* —
  Eternal life continues throughout eternity.

In other words, *eternal life isn't just something that starts after you die.*

*"This is eternal life: that they may know You,
the only true God, and Jesus Christ, whom You have sent."*
(John 17:3 MEV)

HE WHOM THE SON SETS FREE, IS FREE INDEED
FREE FROM ETERNAL DEATH!

5

No Guilt, No Pride,

No Shame!

Then the eyes of both of them were opened,
and they knew...

(Genesis 3:7 NKJV)

Have you ever wondered why animals don't express guilt, pride or shame?
Do you know why they never criticize, judge or deceive?

Animal behaviorists say it's a matter of intelligence, and others believe it's because they have no soul. Both of these opinions are mere speculation at best. Actually, the answer is really quite simple: God made them that way — free from toxic emotions. And what's more important, that's the way God made man — free from toxic emotions. *So, what happened?*

I believe the reason why animals don't struggle with these types of emotions was revealed long ago in the Book of Genesis. The answer was given to us, but we haven't seen it clearly because the truth has been obscured. We've put our focus on minute details and missed the big picture. It's a matter of perspective — like that old expression: *"You can't see the forest for the trees."*

(Note: The meaning of the word "for" is; "because of" or "due to.")

The truth is, we haven't figured out why animals lack certain *human emotions* because we've been focusing on the wrong object — *it's as though there's been a veil over our eyes.*

Even though both man and animals are able to think, feel and express emotions, it is obvious that there is a difference between the *nature* of man and the *nature* of animals.

There's a reason why animals respond the way they do, and *there's a reason* why man responds the way he does, but mere human logic will never figure out why they differ in their responses — *It's because the answer is spiritual!* Without the help of God, no laboratory researcher or behaviorist will ever know *why animals lack certain emotions.*

The answers to these and many other important questions will become obvious once you realize what *did* and *did not* happen in the garden of Eden.

In the previous chapter, *Free from Eternal Death*, I mentioned how God commanded Adam not to eat from the tree of the *knowledge of good and evil* that was located in the midst of the garden. Adam was warned that there would be consequences if he disobeyed but he ignored God's warning and ate from the tree anyway. (See Genesis 2:16-17; 3:6)

This one act of rebellion affected not only Adam but all of creation — *in more ways than we realize.*

The following conversation is what led to the fall of man

Now the serpent was more cunning than any beast of the field
  which the Lord God had made. And he said to the woman,
"Has God indeed said, 'You shall not eat of every tree of the
  garden'?"

And the woman said to the serpent, "We may eat the fruit of the trees
of the garden; but of the fruit of the tree which is in the midst
of the garden,
God has said, 'You shall not eat it, nor shall you touch it,
lest you die.'"

Then the serpent said to the woman, "You will not surely die.
For God knows that in the day you eat of it your *eyes will be opened,*
and you will be like God, knowing good and evil."

So when the woman saw that the tree was good for food,
that it was pleasant to the eyes, and a tree desirable to make one wise,
she took of its fruit and ate. She also gave to her husband with her,
and he ate. Then *the eyes of both of them were opened,* and they knew
that they were naked; and they sewed fig leaves together and made
themselves coverings. (Genesis 3:1-7 NKJV)

Immediately after Adam ate from the forbidden tree, both Adam and Eve's *eyes were opened.* This does not refer to their natural eyes because those were already open, *but rather it refers to their perception and the way they viewed things.* The way they saw themselves had changed, and the way they saw the world was entirely different. Adam and Eve had *opened themselves* up to a knowledge that they were never intended to have. Knowledge that would prove to be detrimental *to all of creation.*

This was not just a tree of the knowledge of evil —
But the knowledge of both good and evil

When I first heard about this tree, the whole idea of it seemed ridiculous. I remember thinking, *if there ever was such a tree, what could possibly be wrong with having knowledge of good and evil?* You might be wondering as well.

I have since learned that what the Bible says is true, even if it seems foolish to the natural mind. (See 1 Corinthians 2:14)

So, before we can understand what harm there could possibly be in having this *knowledge of good and evil*, we must first know *the true nature and love of God.*

It's the love of God that gives us the freedom to choose

To begin with, when God tells us not to do something, it is always for our own good. With regard to the command that God spoke to Adam, it was given for his welfare and protection — *not for his destruction.* The same is true for us today. God told us in His word that *we have the power* to choose life or to choose death.

> I call heaven and earth as witnesses today against you,
> *that* I have set before you life and death, blessing and cursing;
> therefore choose life, that both you and your descendants may live;
> (Deuteronomy 30:19 NKJV)

Adam had the power to choose life, but he willfully chose death. His decision caused an immediate separation from God — *referred to as spiritual death.*

His choice not only affected him and his wife but also the entire human race.

As I previously mentioned, the animals did not experience spiritual death. Due to their innocence, *they were and still are totally exempt from spiritual death.* But this is not the case concerning physical death. *All living beings, including the animals,* will one day have to face physical death because Adam's decision brought a curse to the ground — *physical bodies are made from ground that is still under the curse.*

God knew if Adam's eyes were opened to the knowledge of good and evil, *it would bring forth negative, destructive emotions*. God also knew that if Adam ignored His warning, it would result in death and a cause a curse to come upon the ground.

What happened at the tree that day not only impacted Adam, but it altered the course for the entire creation.

In life there are many choices and God gave us a free will to make our own decisions. But if we ignore His warnings, then what right do we have to blame God for the consequences?

Only a fool ignores warnings from God!

The fool says his heart, "There is no God."
(Psalm 14:1 ESV)

The fear of the Lord is the beginning of knowledge,
But fools despise wisdom and instruction.
(Proverbs 1:7 NKJV)

The consequences of knowing good and evil

The first thing Adam and Eve discovered following their disobedience was that they were naked. They immediately tried to cover themselves because *their perception of their nakedness had changed*. They had known all along that they were naked, but like the other creatures, they had never before been ashamed. The Bible says;

"And they were both naked, the man and his wife, and were not ashamed." (Genesis 2:25 KJV)

Man who was once God-conscious became self-conscious
Animals are not self-conscious

Even though Adam and Eve's nakedness *was not a sin*, their fallen perception of it brought about shame. Even today, nakedness is associated with shame.

Next, we find that fear caused them to hide from God.
God called to Adam and said, "Where are you?"
Adam answered, "I heard Your voice in the garden,
and *I was afraid because I was naked;* and I hid myself."
(See Genesis 3:9-10)

Never before had they been afraid to be naked, and never before did they attempt to hide from God. *Even today man is still hiding from God.* Yet the Bible tells us:

And there is no creature hidden from His sight,
but all things are naked and open to the eyes of Him
to whom we must give account.
(Hebrews 4:13 NKJV)

Both Adam and Eve refused to take ownership of their actions and passed the buck. Adam blamed the woman, and in turn the woman blamed the serpent. If you watch people today, they do the same thing. We blame anyone and everyone for our own sin, and then defend ourselves with a multitude of excuses.

Animals don't play the blame game!

We are all Adam's descendants, consequently we are all born with the same perverted perception. We experience guilt, pride, and shame, simply because our eyes are open to the *knowledge of good and evil.*

**Guilt follows sin, shame follows guilt
You will never see an animal express shame —
because they have no sin to make them to feel guilty**

Animals, on the other hand never ate from the forbidden tree. Consequently, their eyes have never been opened to the knowledge of good and evil. Therefore, they are free from the adverse effects this knowledge brings.

Animals are oblivious to the way we see things. They see everything from a "pre tree perspective" in the same way Adam and Eve did before they ate the forbidden fruit. This explains why animals respond and behave differently than we do. Their perspective comes from a different vantage point — *one of innocence.*

Think about what that means for the animals. They have no comprehension of the kind of knowledge that perverts our way of thinking. It's something that they'll never know and yet it's something that we can't escape — that is, the *knowledge of good and evil.*

It's to their benefit that they don't see things the way we do. That's the reason why animals are never selfish or *self*-conscious. That's why they never plot revenge. And, that's why they're never spiteful, haughty, critical, judgmental or deceptive. Animals do not have the same *awareness* and hang ups that human beings do. They don't understand our toxic, deadly emotions, because they do not respond or react through the knowledge of good and evil. *Only human beings reason along those lines of thought.*

We need to consider that we see the life of an animal through the finite limits of our knowledge and understanding — An understanding that has been framed by the tree of the knowledge of good and evil

As I mentioned earlier, some animal behaviorists will tell you that a dog's intelligence will never exceed that of a two and a half year old child. They say that animals can only feel what *they* refer to as the "basic" emotions — joy, fear, anger and love; and not what *they've* labeled as the more "complex" ones — guilt, pride and shame. To their credit, the behaviorists have admitted that their opinion is *only a hypothesis.*

But just because animals do not experience guilt, pride or shame, along with other toxic emotions, does not mean that they are less intelligent, nor does it prove that they don't have a soul. What it does mean is that animals are *not under the influence of the toxic effects that come from that deadly, forbidden tree.*

Some people say animals don't know right from wrong. This may appear to be true because their evaluation is coming from a human perspective; but again, *it does not mean that they do not have a soul*. Now what animals do lack is the knowledge of good and evil that came to all of mankind through disobedience and sin.

We would have a greater understanding of animals if we recognized that *they are incapable of comprehending life from our twisted point of view*.

Just because both man and animals live in the same world, does not mean that animals are aware of what we are aware of, and vice versa. We only assume that they are.

It would benefit us all if we understood that an *unregenerate man* (a person who is at enmity with God: a lost soul), can only operate through the knowledge of good and evil, while animals on the other hand, navigate from a sinless nature.

We misunderstand animals, because unlike us, their behavior is not influenced by the knowledge of good and evil.

Misunderstood or misbehaving?

People sometimes place ulterior motives onto animals as though they have some sort of hidden agenda for doing the things they do. For example, they may think an animal is angry and trying to get even when nothing could be further from the truth. That is, they believe the animal is acting with a negative purpose when they're not. Balaam's donkey is a perfect example.

If you read the account of what took place in the Book of Numbers, you'll find that Balaam's donkey was trying to protect her owner — not cause him harm. Through ignorance, Balaam beat his donkey when he thought she was being disobedient. Balaam was clueless that his donkey had made a decision to risk her own life in order to save his. *Her motive was altruistic — not rebellious!* (see Numbers 22:22-34)

How many times do we misunderstand the motives of our pets?

If you think you've seen animals express any toxic emotions, *you are mistaken*. It's not possible. The truth is, you've misunderstood what the animal was communicating. You've misinterpreted their reaction or response to *your* behavior.

Again, we often misunderstand the response of an animal to our actions and words because of the way *we* see things. Our perspective of the situation is out of whack. Sometimes we have no clue as to where they're actually coming from, and so we project our human emotions onto them. It's unfair for us to judge what the animals are communicating using knowledge based on the tree of good and evil. To do so, does not take into consideration their vantage point.

Animals cannot *choose* between good and evil. *When animals behave differently than what we expect, it is generally because of a conflict between their God-given natures and our human requirements.*

Let me give you a brief example of what I mean as it pertains to their natural needs: Dog goes to the bathroom on the carpet and not on the newspaper —*in the house!*

> OK, so they've done it a few times and we've told them not to. We come home from work late, and there it is…a puddle on the floor and not the newspaper. We get upset, probably raise our voice and we're obviously angry. Down goes the head and the tail between the legs. It would appear that they are ashamed. No! That's not what's happening.
>
> We need to see the situation from their point of view, and not our distorted perspective, that comes from the knowledge of good and evil.
>
> To them, it is not spiteful, wrong or rebellious to go to the bathroom on the floor. They had to go! They're not trying to be disobedient, we're misreading their intentions. More than likely, they want to please us and see us happy. Their head is down and they are cowering because they know we are upset or angry at them.
>
> How confusing it must be for animals to try and figure us out when they themselves have not been tainted by the deadly tree of knowledge of good and evil.

So, what is their perspective?

Usually, we've locked them up somewhere and then we expect them to do what comes naturally, *in a particular location, and on a certain substance.* Think about it, if you were in their place, and someone locked you up and you had to go, how unreasonable would it be if that someone came home, spanked you, or rubbed your nose in it? If you didn't understand that what you did was *supposedly* wrong, or didn't understand their specific instructions, what would you think, do or feel? *Confused? Hurt? Intimidated?*

Unlike people, animals are not *deliberately* trying to misbehave or rebel. They simply see situations such as these, and many others, far differently than we do.

I believe that we miss it all too often where an animal's behavior is concerned. I could give many more examples, but the point I want to make is this: if you really love animals, then try to understand their perspective on how they see things, especially before you get angry or inappropriately correct them. They're coming from a position of innocence, and then we react from a position based on our knowledge of good and evil.

Again, there are a multitude of things that we do that animals just don't understand, and a lot of what they do we misinterpret. Animals are misunderstood because their perspective is different from ours.

So, where are animals coming from?

Animals don't judge, condemn, or lie, and they don't feel guilt or shame — but they do have love, joy, peace, patience, kindness, goodness, faithfulness, gentleness and self control. In fact, the Bible calls these **attributes**, the "*fruit of the Spirit.*" (See Galatians 5:22, 23 NASB & ESV)

We all know the love and faithfulness of a pet. *Is it possible that animals have the fruit of the Spirit?*

These attributes are what make animals so special

What is fear?

Animals are vulnerable to fear, but did you know that fear is not an emotion? Fear is actually an entity, and the Bible calls it a spirit.

> For God has not given us a *spirit of fear*,
> but of power and of love and of a sound mind.
> (2 Timothy 1:7 NKJV)

Animals can be intimidated by a spirit of fear because they have no authority in the *spirit realm* where fear operates. Therefore, it is the responsibility of believers *to intervene on behalf of the animals by knowing what the Word of God says, and then act accordingly.*

Anger is a manifestation of fear. All anger, with the exception of *righteous anger,* is rooted in fear.

Important Point: What I am about to say is really a topic for another discussion, but I want to bring it to your attention because I feel the subject matter is vitally important. And that is, sometimes there are things that animals do simply because of the demonic influences that have been allowed to operate in and through their lives. Remember, animals have absolutely no authority over the spirit realm. In situations like these we need to ask the question: *how are these spirits gaining access into the animal's life and who has the legal authority to intervene on behalf of the animal?*

If the person in charge of the animal's welfare is oblivious to the strategies of evil in the spirit realm, then the animal will suffer. Not only will that animal suffer but he could also become a danger to others. **MAKE NO MISTAKE:** *demon spirits are real and they are looking for a body to occupy and operate from — both human and animal alike!*

Note: When the Bible talks about the "fear of God," it is *not* talking about the *spirit of fear* mentioned in 2 Timothy 1:7. Godly *fear* is something totally different. It is not a terrorizing spirit; but rather a reverence or piety towards God.

> ...let us have grace, by which we may serve God
> acceptably with reverence and godly fear.
> (Hebrews 12:28 NKJV)

The Bible also tells us, "The fear of the Lord is the beginning of wisdom…"
(Proverbs 9:10 NKJV)

The worst fear of all — the wrath of God!

Beware! There will come a time in the not too distant future, when those who have decided that they *don't* want to have a relationship with a loving God will be subjected to an *intense season of fear*. This fear is not the same as the *reverential fear* of God. But rather, it is a fear that will come upon the wicked when the *wrath of God* is poured out in the last days.

When this happens, evil men will fear a "just" God because their wicked ways will be brought to justice. *They will finally be held accountable for the evil they have done.*

In that season, the Bible tells us that those who have rejected God will be so filled with fear, that they will try to hide themselves from His wrath — *but they will not escape!*

> Then the sky receded as a scroll when it is rolled up,
> and every mountain and island was moved out of its place.
> And the kings of the earth, the great men, the rich men,
> the commanders, the mighty men, every slave and every free man,
> hid themselves in the caves and in the rocks of the mountains,
> and said to the mountains and rocks,
> "Fall on us and hide us from the face of Him who sits on the throne
> and from the wrath of the Lamb!
> *For the great day of His wrath has come,
> and who is able to stand?"* (Revelation 6:14-17 NKJV)

The love and innocence of animals can make a difference

*People with **Autism** and **Asperger Syndrome** often benefit from interacting with animals.*

There is someone in my life who is very special to me. This person has taught me many valuable lessons through the years. My friend is someone who functions at a very high level with Asperger's Syndrome.

When I first met him, I was unaware of spectrum disorders. I knew that he was somehow different, but for a long time I completely misjudged his motives and misunderstood his behavior. *I had been wrong* in the way I responded to his actions because I had totally misread his intentions. Then one day, the Lord showed me where *I had been ignorant,* and finally I understood my friend's perspective.

I can truly say, that I don't know very many people who are as honest and operate on such a high level of integrity as that of my friend, Kenny. He has run a successful business, and I've never known him to lie, mistreat or take advantage of anyone. Even though he keeps to himself, when asked for help, he is always there never expecting anything in return.

One day while I was on the phone with my friend, I asked him what he liked best about the animals. Our conversation was enlightening to say the least.

"All I know is, I like my cats. I like all animals. I don't like people!"

I asked, "Well, why do you like the animals?" He answered, "Because they're not a nasty roach like most people are." I said, "*A nasty roach?*" He answered, "Well, actually a roach is better than most people."

Always amazed by his candid honesty, I asked, "So, what do you like best about them?" He hesitated, and then pensively said, "Well, I can't tell you specifically what I like best about them, Caren. I like them because, you know, they have an effect on me." Not surprised by his answer, I continued on with; "OK, what kind of an effect? A good effect, but what kind of effect?" He quietly responded, "*They get real close to my heart!* I like my cats. I like my cats as much as any human… "

At this point, I wanted to explain where I was coming from, so I said, "I'm trying to find out what it is about an animal that makes people like them, like they do. I have my own thing, but I'm trying to get to the bottom of this. All right, you like them better than people. They're not nasty. You can trust them. But, *what do you like the most about them? Is it their faithfulness? Is it the fact that they're innocent? Is it the fact that they're defenseless? What do you like the most about them?*"

In his straightforward manner he answered and said, "Well, I don't know, it could be all of them. I don't know. I'd have to sit and think on that for a while… I mean, *they are innocent.*"

So, I continued on saying, "And they are defenseless. They never lie."

A bit excited he added, " Well, yeah. That's basically what I said. I like them because, *they're the opposite of people.*"

As I listened on the other end of the phone, I realized that my friend had become distracted by something. When I heard him call out to a kitten to come and get his food — *I knew exactly where he was.*

My friend who has quietly rescued more cats and kittens than anyone I know, had once again driven across town. His mission — to feed and rescue the last abandoned kitten that had been discarded at the dump!

To me, Kenny's sincere and faithful commitment in tending to the needs of so many helpless animals, is a picture of God's heart of compassion and unconditional love.

Many autistic children and adults are drawn to animals rather than people. Studies show that animals significantly increase positive social behaviors in children who have an *autism spectrum disorder.* The value of animals in their lives cannot be denied.

Hospital attendants see remarkable responses from patients who are visited by animals, and the elderly find comfort in having a pet. The reason for this is obvious. Animals have a *sinless nature,* and they don't interact based on perverted toxic emotions that come from the *knowledge of good and evil.*

People who have spectrum disorders, as well as those with other challenges feel safe with animals because they know that they can trust them.

Animals don't put requirements on their friendship. Animals don't put conditions on their love, *and animals never have ulterior motives!*

What happened at the tree of the knowledge of good and evil opened a spiritual "Pandora's box"

What happened at the tree of the knowledge of good and evil changed man, not the animals. It was only man's eyes that were opened to the forbidden knowledge of good and evil. It's important to recognize that we live and interact with a part of God's creation that views things far differently than we do.

Even though the animals still see the world through innocent eyes, *man's sin has affected every aspect of their lives.*

The evil that man's eyes were opened to, has only brought moral *degradation* to the human race. Because we are all descendants of Adam, we are all born with the perverted perception of the knowledge of good and evil, and we act accordingly. Animals don't know what it's like to see from this polluted filter — and *unregenerate man doesn't know what it's like not to!*

I don't believe there's any way we can fully comprehend what it means to have our eyes closed to this forbidden knowledge, any more than we can grasp the timelessness of eternity. Yet we live in a world where the animals suffer at the hand of man's ignorance. We place unreasonable expectations on animals by asking them to respond to the knowledge of good and evil. How can they if they don't see what we see?

The very things that man was never intended to know, the animals still don't know, namely those things that come from the *knowledge of good and evil.*

Animals have emotions too. The difference is, their emotions are not perverted by the knowledge of good and evil.

Animals see things the way man did — before the fall

Everything we do in life involves a choice. Adam was given a choice between two trees right from the beginning; the Tree of Life and the Tree of the Knowledge of Good and Evil. It was a choice between life or death. Adam chose death. So, for the rest of mankind to be redeemed from the consequences of Adams decision, each one of us has been given that same choice — we can either eat from the tree of the knowledge of good and evil, or we can choose Jesus: *Who is the way, the truth and the life.*

Every choice that we make through Him will result in life. Whereas, the decisions we make that are influenced by the tree of the knowledge of good and evil will result in death. God never intended for mankind to partake of this tree nor operate from this knowledge!

**Eternal life is given back to us through Jesus Christ
If we choose Him,
we reconnect back to what was lost in the garden**

Jesus said to him, "I am the way, the truth, and the life.
No one comes to the Father, except through me."
(John 14:6 NKJV)

Why is it important to bring up the tree of the knowledge of good and evil in a book about pets and eternity?

It's important because it reveals the error of those who say out of ignorance that animals are not eternal beings because they don't have the same intelligence as man.

Some even believe that the level of an animal's intelligence is linked to whether or not they have a soul. This is not true. *Intelligence has nothing to do with having a soul.*

Truly, the knowledge that comes from the tree of the knowledge of good and evil is perverted, whereas the knowledge that comes from God is pure.

Animals operate from a different perspective than unregenerate man — that is, they are unable to understand the perverted knowledge that comes from the tree of the knowledge of good and evil. *The knowledge that animals operate from is pure because it comes from God.*

**Animals are not only intelligent–
but they do in fact have a soul**

WHY NO GUILT, NO PRIDE, NO SHAME?

BECAUSE, ANIMALS ARE NOT UNDER THE INFLUENCE
OF THE TREE OF THE KNOWLEDGE OF GOOD AND EVIL!

6

Don't Blame God

"For the Son of Man did not come to destroy
men's lives but to save them."

(LUKE 9:56 NKJV)

God doesn't give you something only to take it away

One Christmas Day, my friend Johnna and I decided to visit St. Augustine
and check out one of America's most historical churches. It looked as
though we had the whole town all to ourselves, that is until we opened

the doors of its quaint little chapel. To our surprise, there were two women at the altar on their knees in prayer.

We waited in the back until they finished, careful not to intrude. Once they stood up, the atmosphere of solemn prayer changed. And suddenly, one of them had become angry, uttering profanities. The other one tried to console her, but that only irritated her all the more. I looked at Johnna and we both knew, *we were there for a reason.*

As we approached them to see if we could help, the woman who was upset poured out her story: "*I didn't want to come here in the first place. I don't want anything to do with God or church!*" Rather stunned I asked, "So then, why *are* you here?" She went on to explain, "I only came here today to make my sister happy. Our parents recently died and she wanted us to come and pay our respects."

I couldn't help but ask, "Why are you mad at God?" Without hesitating she exclaimed, "God killed my cat!"

Surprised by her accusation, I asked, "Where did you ever get the idea that God was the one who killed your cat?"

When she answered, "*from a preacher,*" it felt as though someone had punched me. I couldn't help but think, *no wonder this lady is hurt and angry. Why would anyone say such a thing? And a preacher at that! Are you kidding?* Her cat had been hit by a car and then a preacher tells her, "*If God wanted your cat to live, He would have saved her. She died because it was God's will, and besides, animals are not what's important to God — people are.*"

I've encountered situations similar to this before and they have always affected me in the same way. Touched by her pain and angered by the lies, I was compelled to tell her the truth — *the truth about God, and the truth about her cat.*

As Johnna and I apologized to the lady for the preacher's insensitive and unbiblical remarks, it became obvious to her that we sincerely cared about her and her loss.

6

Don't Blame God

"For the Son of Man did not come to destroy
men's lives but to save them."

(LUKE 9:56 NKJV)

God doesn't give you something only to take it away

One Christmas Day, my friend Johnna and I decided to visit St. Augustine and check out one of America's most historical churches. It looked as though we had the whole town all to ourselves, that is until we opened the doors of its quaint little chapel. To our surprise, there were two women at the altar on their knees in prayer.

We waited in the back until they finished, careful not to intrude. Once they stood up, the atmosphere of solemn prayer changed. And suddenly, one of them had become angry, uttering profanities. The other one tried to console her, but that only irritated her all the more. I looked at Johnna and we both knew, *we were there for a reason.*

As we approached them to see if we could help, the woman who was upset poured out her story: "*I didn't want to come here in the first place. I don't want anything to do with God or church!*" Rather stunned I asked, "So then, why *are* you here?" She went on to explain, "I only came here today to make my sister happy. Our parents recently died and she wanted us to come and pay our respects."

I couldn't help but ask, "Why are you mad at God?" Without hesitating she exclaimed, "God killed my cat!"

Surprised by her accusation, I asked, "Where did you ever get the idea that God was the one who killed your cat?"

When she answered, "*from a preacher,*" it felt as though someone had punched me. I couldn't help but think, *no wonder this lady is hurt and angry. Why would anyone say such a thing? And a preacher at that! Are you kidding?* Her cat had been hit by a car and then a preacher tells her, "*If God wanted your cat to live, He would have saved her. She died because it was God's will, and besides, animals are not what's important to God — people are.*"

I've encountered situations similar to this before and they have always affected me in the same way. Touched by her pain and angered by the lies, I was compelled to tell her the truth — *the truth about God, and the truth about her cat.*

As Johnna and I apologized to the lady for the preacher's insensitive and unbiblical remarks, it became obvious to her that we sincerely cared about her and her loss.

I knew that it wasn't God's will for her cat to die, so how could I stand by and watch her run from God because some ill-informed preacher portrayed Him to be something He's not? Too many others have already gone to a lost eternity because they believed in a religious, institutionalized God.

This lady had been misled about her cat and misled about God. She needed to know the truth.

Then came the pivotal moment when she asked that crucial question, "Can you tell me where my cat is?" Without hesitating, I answered her with a resounding — YES! Barriers immediately came down and I knew I had her undivided attention.

When Johnna and I explained to her that God's love for her cat was far greater than her own, she was surprised. I knew it was important for her to understand that love is not something God has, but rather, love is who He is. It was obvious that the truth about His love was totally contrary to everything she had ever heard or believed. (See 1 John 4:8)

Then as I went on and shared God's plan of redemption for the animals, I recognized a change in her countenance. It was obvious — *hope replaced despair.* Her eyes filled with tears as she thought about her own destiny. It was then that I was able to tell her all that Jesus had done for her.

Once the truth was revealed and the lies were exposed, she no longer saw God as being cruel or evil. I could see a transformation in her countenance, and she was no longer the angry woman we had first encountered. She had experienced a heart change.

The love of God can heal even the most broken of hearts! (See Psalm 147:3)

If God is not to blame, then who is?

Why do so many people believe that God is the one who is wreaking havoc on creation and causing all of their problems?

It's not complicated, it's because we have an enemy who is the master of **deception**. Jesus not only called him a liar, but said that he is the father of all lies. (See John 8:44)

Our enemy is ruthless, cunning, divisive, and again, the master of deception. He is a fallen angel and commonly referred to as the Devil or Satan. The Bible reveals his true identity in the book of Revelation:

> So the great dragon was cast out, that serpent of old,
> **called the Devil and Satan**, who **deceives** the whole world;
> he was cast to the earth, and his angels were *cast out* with him.
> (Revelation 12:9 NKJV)

Satan has an invisible army and it is more sophisticated than any military structure the world has ever known. Just as the United States Armed Forces is made up of different branches, so is Satan's army. He's the Commander in Chief, and his officers along with the members of his rank and file consist of *fallen angels*. Along with his *cohorts*, he strategically plans and executes attacks against you and your family, *as well as your pets.*

THE SUPERNATURAL REALM

Make no mistake, whether you realize it or not, there is an unseen war raging against you. If you don't understand what's going on in the realm of the supernatural — *you will be deceived.* Satan may even work through your family members and friends to get to you and your pets.

Most people are blind to the fact that they are in the midst of an invisible war. They never realize that the attacks coming against them are actually orchestrated by Satan's army. I personally once believed that the devil was no more than a cartoon character, a figment of Hollywood's imagination. *Boy, was I ever duped! I only wish I had known the truth about him sooner.*

The truth is, the devil is not some *made up* character with horns, carrying a pitchfork and wearing a red suit. *He is for real,* and the Bible says that he masquerades as an *angel of light*. (See 2 Corinthians 11:14 NKJV)

Along with his many cohorts, Satan operates from the invisible *supernatural realm*. Just because you cannot see him or his army, doesn't mean they aren't real. You can't see electricity either, but try putting your hand on a high voltage line and watch what happens.

What people don't realize is that the *supernatural realm* coexists with and runs parallel to our *natural realm*. Everything happening in the natural world is the result of things that are taking place in the spirit world. The two worlds coincide and they are connected. Nothing just happens! There are no coincidences!

Satan and his army of *fallen angels* plan strategic attacks against you. With the help of the Lord, and by understanding Satan's tactics, schemes and weapons, *you can prevail!*

But, it's imperative that you be informed because — *ignorance is not bliss!* Despite the catchy cliché that Thomas Gray coined in his poem claiming "ignorance is bliss," the Bible warns us not to be ignorant.

> Lest Satan should take advantage of us;
> for we are not **ignorant** of his devices. (2 Corinthians 2:11 NKJV)

To be ignorant means we lack essential knowledge. The Bible says, *"My people are destroyed for lack of knowledge."* (Hosea 4:6 NKJV)

So if you don't want Satan taking advantage of you, then make it your business to know and understand what God has to say about Satan's devices. Should you ever find yourself in a situation where the enemy is out to destroy you or your pets, remember — *ignorance is not bliss!*

Again, the Bible warns us about this ruthless enemy:

> Be sober, be vigilant; because your *adversary*
> the devil walks about like a roaring lion,
> seeking whom he may devour.
> (1 Peter 5:8 NKJV)

Think about this; *if God were to blame, would He warn us?*

Jesus said it all in John 10:10;

The thief does not come except to steal,
and to kill, and to destroy.
I have come that they may have life,
and that they may have it more abundantly. (NKJV)

How much clearer does it need to be? It should be obvious to anyone who reads the Bible, that God is not the one to blame for the death of anyone's pet or family member. He explicitly tells us in His word that He is the One who *gives life* and that *death is His enemy.* (See 1 John 5:11 and 1 Corinthians 15:25-26 NKJV)

Death is an enemy of God!

Many people are convinced that it was God who brought death to creation, but that is not what the Bible says. *Death gained its access through man's sin, not through the will of God.*

Death is not only *repugnant* to the nature of all living creatures, but death is also repugnant to God. Death is the foe and the devil is the one who is out to kill! The following verses make it clear that Satan is the one who does the killing and God is the only One who gives life.

…that through death He might destroy him
who *had the power of death, that is, the devil…*
(Hebrews 2:14 NKJV)

"The last enemy that shall be destroyed is death." — It shall cease to be!
(1Corinthians 15:26; Revelation 21:4 NKJV)

The Bible does not teach that *death* itself is to be *vanquished* by Christ — that would mean that death would simply be *defeated.* BUT NO, the Bible tells us that *death is to be utterly destroyed by Christ,* in other words — *death shall cease to be!*

We can know four things about death from the verse above:

Death is an enemy
Death is the last enemy

Death is an enemy to be destroyed
Death is the last enemy that shall be destroyed!

If God were the cause of death — would He defeat death?

Remember that Jesus Himself said,

The **thief** does not come except to steal, and **to kill**, and to destroy.
I have come that they may have life,
and that they may have it more abundantly.
(John 10:10 NKJV)

If you can't identify your enemy, how will you win the war?

Blaming God is a primary tactic of the enemy. If you play into his hands and take the bait, it could cost you everything. The enemy knows that if he can convince you that God is your problem, you will never seek God's help. *You place not only yourself, but your pets as well in a vulnerable position when you blame God.* God wants to help you, but when you blame Him you block His protection.

Rejecting God's protection!

When the events of 9/11 took place, everybody was talking about God. One newscaster said, "*Well, where was God when this happened?*"

The answer is, where everybody put Him: Outside! Out of their schools, out of their government, and out of their lives!

It's insane to go around complaining about why God isn't doing something if you've kicked Him out of your life

The truth is, God wants us all to be under His *umbrella of protection.* But if we choose to reject Him, then we have stepped out from under His protection. So when the storms of life come, we may suffer the consequences and possibly jeopardize the safety of our family and pets.

How Satan lies to people

The first time someone told me that Satan was a liar, I was baffled. I thought, how can someone I can't see or hear lie to me?

You may not realize this, but not all of your thoughts are your own. The Bible tells us that the devil and his cohorts have the ability to put thoughts into our minds. In other words, not all of what we think originates with us. Satan knows that the thoughts we dwell on will ultimately determine our destiny.

For instance, if he can get you to believe thoughts of fear, doubt or unbelief, he knows you'll eventually speak them out. If you speak them out, you give him a legal right to bring those things to pass. Conversely, if you speak words of life and blessing from God's word, *God can bring those words to come to pass.*

You choose your own future by the thoughts you speak

It's important to understand that the enemy is constantly bombarding us with thoughts that cause wrong believing and consequently wrong decisions. Unfortunately, most people are totally oblivious to what's actually happening.

Satan systematically assaults us with thoughts and suggestions that provoke us to say or do something that will aid in his operation. The Apostle Paul referred to these thoughts as "*fiery darts.*" He told us to extinguish each and every dart by using the shield of faith.

…above all, taking the shield of faith
with which **you** will be able to quench all the fiery darts of the wicked one.
(Ephesians 6:16 NKJV)

No one is exempt from attacks of the "fiery darts." The problem is that most people are oblivious to what is happening. They have no idea that their mind is Satan's battlefield.

Satan and his cohorts *cannot read our minds.* However, we give them the ability to deduce what we're thinking by what we say and what we do. That's why it's important to pay attention to what we think, and watch what we say because:

Death and life are in the power of the tongue.
(Proverbs 18:21 NKJV)

 Eternity with Your Pets

Is God in control?

No! God gave man a free will and the right to choose. If God was in control, we wouldn't have a free will.

The most important example of man's free will is his right to choose where he will spend eternity. Some believe that they have no say in the matter, but that's not true. Make no mistake. God set the rules but He gave man the right to choose.

It is your decision as to whether you receive or reject Jesus Christ as your personal Savior. This puts *you* directly in control of *your* eternal destiny. If *you* chose to reject Jesus, *don't blame God* for the result of *your* decision.

It is written,

> "I have set before *you* life and death,
> blessing and cursing; therefore *choose* life,
> that both you and your descendants may live;"
> (Deuteronomy 30:19 NKJV)

GOD IS SOVEREIGN!

When we say that God is *sovereign*, we're referring to the fact that He is paramount and supreme. There is no one higher in authority or power. *This does not mean that God controls everything.* People have been confused because *religion* portrays the sovereignty of God to mean that nothing happens outside of what He wills or allows. This is a false assumption because, in truth, *God has subjected Himself to His word!*

> The Lord is not slack concerning His promise,
> as some count slackness, but is long-suffering toward us,
> **not willing** that any should perish but that all should
> come to repentance. (2 Peter 3:9 NKJV)

The words in the above verse epitomize the sovereignty of God.

Then who is in control?

This world is in a mess; and it all resulted from what happened in the garden. Adam originally had all authority, but his decision to follow

Satan allowed Satan to become the *"god of this world."* (See 2 Corinthians 4:4 KJV)

At this very moment Satan is controlling the world system through those who follow him — some people follow him even unknowingly. But Satan's legal authority is only temporary, and for a very short time. Why? Because, *"The earth is the Lord's, and all its fullness, the world and those who dwell therein."* (Psalm 24:1 NKJV)

The good news is this: *Satan's lease as the "god of this world," is about to expire!*

Why doesn't God do something?

He did — 2000 years ago!

Everything Adam lost, Jesus regained on the cross at Calvary. Even though there is still a temporary lease under Satan's control, Jesus has once and for all regained the keys of the Kingdom. *Anyone* who receives Jesus as their personal Lord and Savior has access to those keys. This is how the plan of God is legally executed on the earth — *through God's covenant people.*

So when people say things like, "The devil can only do what God allows him to do," they don't know what they're talking about. That's not what the Scriptures say. The Scriptures say that the devil does what WE allow him to do. Jesus' brother James said:

> "… submit to God. Resist the devil and he will *flee from you."*
> (James 4:7 NKJV)

If we neglect to use the authority that God has given us, *we're* the ones who allow the devil to do his evil works.

You're either on God's side or the devil's — There is no demilitarized zone!

God is not orchestrating the wickedness of people, and He is not in partnership with Satan. Man with his free will chooses to cooperate with Satan and his *minions,* or he chooses to cooperate with God and His angels. The choice is ours. *If we don't take a stand, then by default we have chosen Satan — the enemy of God.*

You must be aware that there is no **demilitarized zone***!* You're either on God's side, or Satan's side.

If God were in control

If God's will were controlling this world, it would be a different place. There would be no sin, no sickness, no hunger or death *and no one would go to hell.*

If God were in control, the world would be a perfect place. There would be no animal abuse, no child molestation, no rapes, no murders, etc. In other words, there would be no evil.

God will never leave you defenseless!

The Bible says, that those who are strong in the Lord and in the power of His might will be able to stand against the wiles of the devil when they put on the whole *"armor" of God.* (See Ephesians 6:10 NKJV) So what does it mean to, *"be strong in the Lord and the power of His might?"*

It means that you put your trust in God and His Word and believe that He is with you in your battles. (See Proverbs 3:5,6)

There is a big difference between being strong, and being strong in the Lord, even though they may appear to be the same thing. (See 2 Corinthians 12:9) The first focuses on what I can do for myself. The second is more powerful because it is a conscious choice to exercise confidence in what God has already done for me through Christ Jesus.

This second kind of strength does not depend on my physical skill, talent or ability, *but the power of God working through me.* It means I "rest" in Him with a confidence that He cannot fail. (See Proverbs 3:5,6; Joel 3:10c; 1 John 4:4; Philippians 4:13)

Is *divine intervention* available for our pets?

Yes, but it requires a relationship with God through prayer. Relationship with God is vital! Everything your pet will ever need is available, when you are in covenant with God. Whether its health, provision or protection, find out what God said in His written word and pray in agreement with Him. When you do, you give God the legal right to intervene on your pet's behalf.

No one is good but One, that is, God.
(Mark 10:18 NKJV)

If you've ever had something happen to one of your animals remember, ***don't blame God!*** It is never His will for your pets to be harmed in any way. Bad things happen when man exercises his free will in cooperation with Satan's schemes. Whether it's sickness, death or any other horrific calamity, God is never the cause.

God said death is His enemy, therefore death can't be His will. If it steals, if it kills and if it destroys — it's from the devil! **If it restores, if it gives life and if it redeems — it's of God.**

There should be no doubt about *who is for you and who is against you.* It is God's plan to give you a future and a hope.

For I know the thoughts that I think toward you,
says the Lord, thoughts of peace and not of evil,
to give you a future and a hope.
(Jeremiah 29:11)

IF GOD IS FOR US, WHO CAN BE AGAINST US?
(Romans 8:31 NKJV)

7

Unconditional Love

"I will never leave you nor forsake you"

(HEBREWS 13:5 NKJV)

Before I knew God, there was a moment in time when life seemed hopeless and not worth living. It felt as though I had been caught up in the eye of a tornado, spun around and thrown to the ground like scattered debris. *I've had disappointments before, but nothing like this.*

The anguish of a betrayal, a divorce, financial ruin, the loss of my ranch, along with the death of several pets — all hit me at the same time.

Seemingly left with no other options, I moved with my animals three thousand miles away from my dreams. Devastated and alone, my life was in a state of turmoil!

I wanted to pick up the pieces and put my life back together, but I just didn't know how. I've always been a positive person, so I did what was logical and began by reading a popular self-help book.

While sitting cross legged on my living room floor with the book in my lap, I flipped through the pages hoping to find an answer that would fix my life. It wasn't long before I sensed a strange, *ominous* presence that seemed to permeate the atmosphere. *That's when the real battle began.*

In my darkest hour, with my head down and my face in my hands, I started to weep. Feelings of failure, hopelessness and despair overwhelmed me. From out of nowhere, my mind was relentlessly bombarded with one crazy thought after another. Thoughts like, *I'll never recover, and it really doesn't matter to anyone if I live or die.*

It wasn't long before those thoughts turned into suggestions of how to end it all. Then two options came to mind — the use of a .38 Special or an overdose of sleeping pills.

Looking back at the situation, it was as though I had been hypnotized. Part of me was saying, *this is insane! You've never thought anything like this before.* Yet another part of me was saying, *it's the 'only way out of your hopeless situation. Just end the pain!* (Read about fiery darts in the "Don't Blame God" chapter.)

What happened next, I will remember for the rest of my life

It was as though I had been caught up into another realm. I was unaware of my environment and in a stupor when I heard something inside of me say, *"Look up!"*

Almost supernaturally, my head lifted. My eyes immediately became fixed on three small puppies who were curled up together sound asleep.

Semilla and Bello several months later.

Then I remembered — *there were also six horses and four cats who were waiting outside.* It was a wake-up call for me!

Suddenly I thought, *what would happen to them if I would have taken my life?* That's when reality set in. How could I have ever been so selfish? Who would be there to take care of them? And even more importantly, what about their love for me? There was no doubt that I loved my animals, but how could I ever deny their love for me — it was unconditional. *What right did I have to abandon them?*

The event that changed me forever

With tears streaming down my face, I let out the most fervent cry of my life, *"God, I can't even kill myself!"*

Now, I wasn't blaming God for my situation because somehow I knew He wasn't the problem, but I still felt trapped. My circumstances were so overwhelming that I remember thinking, *how much lower can I go? I don't even have the option of taking my life!*

Then suddenly from out of nowhere, I heard a voice that is impossible to describe. It was audible and unlike any other voice I had ever heard. The only way I can describe this voice is to say that it sounded as if it came from another dimension. It shook the very atmosphere. There was no doubt, it was the voice of God. He said, *"Caren, I love you! I will never leave you, nor forsake you!"*

I knew nothing about God, but I knew that God had just spoken to me!

My desperate cry to God that day initiated the greatest event of my life — My salvation

There was an immediate transformation in me as well as the entire atmosphere. The ominous spirit that had been present instantly disappeared, and the room was filled with a peace unlike anything I had ever experienced before. It was as though liquid love had been poured over me. *I had had a touch from God!*

Every bit of fear and anxiety was gone. Although nothing had changed with my natural circumstances, somehow I knew everything was going to work out right. *After all, God had just spoken to me.* And not only did He speak, His words changed my life forever.

Now I wasn't quite sure what the word *forsake* meant. My guess would have been there was no difference in the meaning between *leave* and *forsake*.

It was vitally important for me to understand what God was saying, so I looked up the words and compared the two. **FORSAKE** means to renounce, abandon, desert, leave stranded or turn your back on. **LEAVE** means to depart or go away from.

Several months later I was *born again* and began reading the Bible. I discovered that what God had said to me audibly on that day was also in His written word. Wow! *"I will never leave you nor forsake you."* (Hebrews 13:5; Joshua 1:5)

Previously, I had no knowledge of His promise because I had never read the Bible or been to a church. But suddenly I understood — *God loved me even when I was living a life of sin.* And He loved me enough to never give up on me.

When we cry out from our inner most being for God to help us, He will always show up. It doesn't matter what we've done. If our heart is desperate for God to deliver us, He will. That's exactly what He did for me that day when I was headed down a path of destruction with Satan leading the way. If I would have followed the devil's plan for my life, my very next moment would have been a hell worse than the hell I was experiencing on earth.

So, that day when Satan was planning to take my life, God stepped in and revealed His unconditional love for me through the unconditional love of my animals.

My animals were the bridge that connected me to the Lord!

Agape love — the greatest force in the universe

And now abide faith, hope, love, these three;
but the greatest of these is **love.**
(1 Corinthians 13:13 NKJV)

Love is one of the most misunderstood words in our society. It has been distorted, redefined and perverted. When the Bible refers to the love of God, it is talking about *agape* love.

The Greek words eros, philia and storge are also words for love but they have a different meaning than the word *agape*. For instance, *Eros* is used when referring to romance or sexual love. *Philia* indicates friendship or brotherly love, and *storge* means familial love like that of a parent.

Agape is a Greek word that means *unconditional* love. This love is unique and different, because it is divine and represents God's eternal covenant.

Agape love is the greatest force in the universe because God is Agape love!

What is agape love?

Agape love is selfless, sacrificial, committed, forgiving and non-judgmental. It is not based on performance, feelings or chemistry. It's a love *by choice*, an act of the will. Agape love is benevolent.

The Apostle Paul best described agape love when he wrote:

Love suffers long and is kind; love does not envy;
love does not parade itself, is not puffed up;
does not behave rudely, does not seek its own,
is not provoked, thinks no evil; does not rejoice in iniquity,
but rejoices in the truth; bears all things,
believes all things, hopes all things, endures all things.
(1 Corinthians 13:4-7 NKJV)

Animals show us the true characteristics of agape love!

Does God love the animals?

God's relationship with the animals is eternal and He expresses His love through His covenants. A covenant is an understanding between all parties involved. It wouldn't be a covenant if one of the parties didn't understand. And when God makes a covenant, it is an eternal promise!

God promised to make a New Covenant in the future with both man and animal.

In that day I will make a **covenant** for them
With the beasts of the field,
With the birds of the air,
And with the creeping things of the ground.
Bow and sword of battle I will shatter from the earth,
To make them lie down safely. (Hosea 2:18 NKJV)

The fact that God would enter into a covenant with the animals, is evidence of His love for them

Immediately after the flood, God had made a covenant with Noah *and the animals.* Seven times in the book of Genesis, God included the animals in His covenant. Every time He made a promise to man, He made the same promise to the animals. Again, when God makes a covenant it's an everlasting promise. (See Genesis quote below)

Animals have a covenant relationship with God, and they understand His covenant

"As for me,
I am establishing my covenant with you and your
descendants after you, **and with every living creature
that is with you**, the birds, the domestic animals, and
every animal of the earth with you, as many
as came out of the ark…when I bring clouds over the
earth and the bow is seen in the clouds, I will remember
my covenant that is between me and you
and every living creature of all flesh;
and the waters shall never again become a flood to destroy
all flesh. When the bow is in the clouds, I will see it
and remember the **everlasting covenant** between God and
every living creature of all flesh that is on the earth."
God said to Noah, "**This is the sign of the covenant
that I have established between me and all flesh that
is on the earth.**"
(Genesis 9:9-10, 14-17 NRSV)

Would God make an everlasting covenant with the animals if they were not eternal?

In the final words of the book of Jonah, we see again that the heart of God is to save the animals

And should I not pity Nineveh, that great city,
in which are more than one hundred and twenty
thousand persons who cannot discern between
their right hand and their left — *and much livestock?*
(Jonah 4:11 NKJV)

Animals are valuable to God, and God said they should be valuable to us.

The following is God's instruction on how He expects us to treat the animals.

> A righteous man regards the life of his animal,
> But the tender mercies of the wicked are cruel.
> (Proverbs 12:10 NKJV)

When we look at what that verse actually means, God's position regarding the value of the life of an animal becomes clear. The word **REGARD** means: to love, guard, protect, hold in high esteem, show respect — and tend to the needs of the animal. (Webster 1828)

A **RIGHTEOUS** person is someone who is just and lawful. They are in *right standing* with God.

Therefore, Proverbs 12:10, could be translated to say: *A person who is in right standing with God, loves, guards, protects, holds in high esteem, respects and tends to the **soul** (nephesh) of his animal.*

If a righteous man regards the life of his animal, then someone who doesn't look after, or tend to the needs of his animal, would be considered unrighteous or cruel. Most importantly, a righteous man understands that animals have a special place in God's Kingdom.

According to the Bible— True Christianity is not harmful to animals

God Himself watches over the birds and takes care of them

Jesus said:

> Look at the birds of the air,
> for they neither sow nor reap nor gather into barns;
> yet your heavenly Father feeds them.
> (Matthew 6:26 NKJV)

When we feed the birds, we are serving God.

Jesus tells us again that God loves and takes care of His animals:
"Are not two sparrows sold for a penny?
And not one of them will fall to the ground without your Father."
(Matthew 10:29 MEV)

Animals are not just a random after thought, but a prime concern to God

Did you know that God also included the animals in the Sabbath rest? In the book of Exodus we find the Ten Commandments. The fourth commandment was God's instruction to His people to include the animals, as they kept the Sabbath day holy.

"Remember the Sabbath day, to keep it holy.
Six days you shall labor and do all your work,
but the seventh day is the Sabbath of the Lord your God.
In it you shall do no work: you, nor your son,
nor your daughter, nor your male servant,
nor your female servant, nor your *cattle*,
nor your stranger who is within your gates." (Exodus 20:8-10 NKJV)

Then it's repeated again;

"Six days you shall do your work,
and on the seventh day you shall rest,
that your ox and your donkey may rest,
and the son of your female servant
and the stranger may be refreshed." (Exodus 23:12 NKJV)

Noah's ark provided for the preservation of the animals

Just about everyone has heard of the account where Noah spent years building an ark with no sign of rain. That was God's plan, and a major part of that plan included the preservation of the animals.

Why was Noah instructed to make the ark taller than a building three stories high? Did he need a boat that big to save only eight people? No! God also had the animals in His heart.

It was God who commanded Noah to take the animals and the birds.

And it was God who engineered the ark to accommodate the animals for the purpose of preserving them. (See Genesis 6:18-21)

...O Lord, You preserve man and beast.

(Psalm 36:6 NKJV)

God's plan for the ark demonstrates His love for mankind, as well as the animals, proving that it is His will for *all of creation to be saved.* Since God does not change, we can trust that His plan remains the same today and for all of eternity.

"For I am the Lord, I change not..." (Malachi 3:6 KJV)

Why do we find more references to animals in the Old Testament than we do in the New Testament?

Most references in the Bible regarding animals are found in the Old Testament. These are foundational Scriptures and they provide valuable knowledge that helps to give a better understanding of the New Testament.

God's principles regarding the relationship of man to the animals has not changed from the Old Testament to the New Testament. Again, God has not changed His mind about how man should relate to the animals.

In the Old Testament, we find God instructing man to care for and protect His animals. Within those instructions, it is evident that God Himself has the highest regard for each and every one of them.

In the New Testament, nothing has changed regarding God's position. If anything, *there is an even greater expectation on man and a higher level of accountability concerning the welfare of animals.*

In the New Testament, it is expected that we not only understand our responsibility towards them, but also recognize that we will one day answer to God for our *stewardship* where the animals are concerned.

Each of the previous passages of the Bible tells us that animals are valuable to God. As their caretakers, *man is expected to protect and tend to the needs of the animals in such a way that is pleasing to God.*

God not only expects us to care about what He cares about, but the Scriptures are clear — *God is unwavering about the welfare of His animals.*

Do animals love unconditionally?

If you have animals, you already know the answer is *yes*. In fact, animals not only give love but they also need love.

My first experience with unconditional love came from my pets. They loved me no matter what. This is because God has given the animals an ability to *empathize* with what we are feeling, and then act accordingly. I can honestly say, the love of my animals has never failed me. (See 1 Corinthians 13:8 NKJV)

What makes animals so special?

The answer is simple. Animals are divinely connected to God because they are sinless. They receive love from God and then give love to us. This precious and unconditional love can only come from God.

Have you ever felt as though you would rather be with animals than people? The reason this is true for so many is because animals have a sinless nature and the ability to love unconditionally. Whether people realize it or not, they are actually searching for the love of God. Since animals are directly connected to God, through them we can experience what it's like to receive His unconditional love.

True *agape* or *unconditional love*, can only originate from God.

How can someone give love if they don't have love?

Agape love is a fruit of the Spirit. The Bible tells us:

> *...the fruit of the Spirit is love, joy, peace, longsuffering, kindness, goodness, faithfulness, gentleness, self control...*
> (Galatians 5:22, 23 NKJV)

Animals exhibit the fruit of the Spirit!

This does not mean that the Holy Spirit lives inside of animals. There is no need for the Holy Spirit to live on the inside of an animal — there has never been a separation of fellowship between God and the animals. Broken fellowship between God and man, came through Adam's sin. The Holy Spirit came to live in man *after what Jesus accomplished through the cross.*

Drifter

Spanky's love for Drifter continues on

Tragically, my German shepherd, Drifter, was run over by a truck and killed. Her very best friend was one of my cats named Spanky. For weeks after the incident, Spanky sat crying on the exact spot where the accident took place. She was so distraught that if I even mentioned Drifter's name in her presence, she would let out a gut wrenching, heart breaking cry.

There are many reports of animals who will not leave the grave site of the one they love. It is apparent that animals mourn and feel pain just like we do when a loved one is gone.

Spanky

The death of a person or animal does not end the love felt by the one left behind. What I'm saying is; the animal left behind does not stop loving just because the person or animal they love is no longer with them. Truly, we all are eternal beings, and even the temporary separation by death cannot end true agape love for one another. **Agape love is eternal!**

LOVE IS TIMELESS — LOVE IS ENDLESS — LOVE IS FOREVER — LOVE NEVER FAILS

Unconditional love from animals in the "wild"

A great example of unconditional love was demonstrated in the reunion of Christian the Lion and two Australian men.

The story begins when the young men adopted Christian as a cub. But as time passed, they recognized how vital it was for their young adult lion to be released into the wild — *for his own welfare.*

And so it happened that Christian was set free and separated from what he knew to be family. Later on we discover through their heartwarming reunion that *he never forgot the bond of love that existed between himself and the men who raised him.* Even though Christian was free in the wilds of Africa and beginning a family of his own, he never forgot and he never stopped loving the men who loved him.

Another example of unconditional love is found in the unique relationships between Kevin Richardson and the wild animals of South Africa. It is obvious that his relationships are intimate, pure and God-like — *without a doubt, supernatural!* (Kevin Richardson is also known as, "The Lion Whisperer.")

Both examples give us an understanding of the personal relationships that Adam must have had with the animals before the fall.

The videos of both Kevin Richardson and Christian the Lion, provide proof that unconditional love *does exist between man and animals in the "wild."*

I believe that both man and animals were given the ability to love because they are eternal beings. God's love is eternal.

————————

**You receive unconditional love from your pet —
Their love cannot save you**

**But, if you receive unconditional love from the Lord,
He will give you eternal life**

Does God love unconditionally?

Each and every one of us has an *innate* need to be loved unconditionally. We all have a void on the inside, and that void can only be filled by God.

Some people believe that we have to be holy in order for God to love us or to answer our prayers. Not so! *We can't do anything* to make God love us any more than He already does. He loves us no matter what!

Going to church and doing good deeds does not make God love anyone. God places no conditions on His love, but what He does place a condition on is how we can receive eternal salvation. Eternal salvation cannot be earned, it can only be obtained by accepting Jesus Christ and the *finished work of the cross*.

No one goes to heaven because of their good works!

God cannot look the other way and ignore it if we reject the sacrifice of His Son, Jesus. But, even if we choose to reject Jesus Christ as our personal Savior, God will still love us unconditionally. God's love has nothing to do with who we are, but everything to do with who HE is. Love is not something God does, God is LOVE!

> And we have known and believed the love that God has for us.
> God is love, and he who abides in love abides in God,
> and God in him.
> (1 John 4:16 NKJV)

How can we know for sure that God's love for us is unconditional?

Because of what Jesus did for us on the cross at Calvary.

Note: Even though God is love, those who have had a poor example of love from an earthly father may have a difficult time relating to God's love.

Do not judge God by your own human relationships

The more you understand God's love, the freer you will be. Nothing can harm you when you know His love. It's a hedge around you — a barrier the enemy can't get through. *That's why love never fails.* (See 1 Corinthians 13:8 NKJV)

Again, even though your pet's love for you is unconditional, their love cannot give you salvation. Only God and His unconditional love can give you salvation and eternal life.

Love has everything to do with eternity

We all have a God-void that can only be filled by receiving God's love. Agape love is eternal, selfless and unconditional. Your pet's love is merely a snapshot of God's agape love. The love we receive from the animals *can only come from God* and is further evidence that they are eternal.

Beloved, let us love one another for love is of God,
and everyone who loves is born of God and knows God.
(1 John 4:7, 12, 16)

And now, Let me say to you, what God once said to Me…

"Just open your heart and receive My love.
You know how to do that with the animals.
You receive their love and attention every day.
You trust them, now trust Me.
That's a picture of what I want from you."

The message is clear

The heart of God is for us to know and understand His love for all of creation.

People may not believe that God loves the animals but they oftentimes don't believe He loves them either. His message is clear — He restores all who love Him. Those who really don't love Him will turn away, and those who don't know Him must be told. *God's animals know and love Him!*

The truth is, there is no reason for the animals to be justified any more than the earth needs to be justified. *Only man needs justification — it's that simple.* Those who choose God will enjoy eternal life with the animals and those who don't — *will have chosen eternal destruction.* In any case, all of God's animals will return to Him — *God's covenant protects the innocent!*

While it is true that God said He would never leave nor forsake us, *this does not mean that we will not leave or forsake Him.* We have a free will and the love of God must be *received* in order to obtain eternal salvation. (See Deuteronomy 30:19 and John 1:12; 3:16, 17)

Without receiving God's love, there is no reconciliation. Without reconciliation, there can be no eternal salvation. And the only way to receive eternal salvation, is by accepting Jesus Christ as your Lord and Savior!

"Now all these things are from God, who reconciled us to Himself through Christ and gave us the ministry of reconciliation..."
(2 Corinthians 5:18 NASB)

UNCONDITIONAL LOVE SAYS;
"I WILL NEVER LEAVE YOU NOR FORSAKE YOU"
(Hebrews 13:5 NKJV)

8

Why the Innocent?

Greater love has no one than this, than to lay
down one's life for his friends.

(JOHN 15:13 NKJV)

I was surprised when I discovered that there was a time when animals were required by God to be sacrificed. *Why would God ever want such a horrific thing to be done?*

You may wonder why I would bring up such a gruesome subject as *animal sacrifices* in a book about pets and eternity. I'll explain, but first let me say that this was not an easy subject for me to explore. I had to work past the heartache and emotions — just to do the research.

My closest friends know me as someone extremely sensitive to the feelings of animals, especially when pain and suffering are involved. It's to the point that almost all animal movies and shows are *off limits* for me. In most scripts it seems like there's always a "Lassie" or "War Horse" who ends up in some unfortunate or heartbreaking situation, usually one I just can't watch. Even though I've been told many times that the ending usually turns out okay, I still can't bear the sad scenes in between. That's just me and I've come to know my compassion for animals is extreme. I accept and embrace that part of me because I now know that it was God who made me this way — *for His purpose.*

I remember when I first learned that animal sacrifices were required under the **Old Covenant**. I was heartsick! For a long time I had decided to just ignore the subject and pretend that they had never taken place. This was definitely one topic that I never wanted to think about, let alone confront. There was nothing that seemed more wrong to me than the sacrificing of animals. But even so, I knew in my heart that God was a good God and someday it would all sort itself out and somehow make sense.

Then one night in Tampa, Florida I was trapped! While sitting in a Bible class I *had* to listen because it was required; there was no way out. The topic — *Animal Sacrifices*! I remember how much it took me off guard and shook me to the core. The pain of it all literally started a flood of tears that nearly blinded me on the 90 plus mile ride home. I'll never forget the fervent cries that I hollered out to God from inside my truck, while outside heaven's relentless tears splashed against my windshield.

"Why!" I asked, "Why the innocent!
What did they ever do to deserve that?"

That's what I screamed out to God in one of my life's most agonizing moments. I questioned, how could anything so unfair be done to the innocent animals, at the request of a loving God?

With every fiber of my being it seemed wrong and cruel and now I was confronted with it — head on. I knew this was a defining moment for me, and I realized how important it was to understand from God's perspective *why* sacrifices had to be done. I had the opinions and teachings of others, but inside I knew there was more.

One thing I've learned over the years is that when you get serious with God about something, you don't have to look very far for Him — or the answer. There are times when His response is immediate, and I was elated that this was one of those times.

He heard every word that night, and His love filled my heart and soul with more compassion than I could ever begin to describe. His peace calmed my heart in such a way that no words can describe.

My tears stopped when I heard Him say, "I know how you feel. I feel the very same way. That's how I felt when My innocent Son was made a sacrifice for *you*. I felt the torment and suffering that He endured, as well as the torment and suffering of *every* innocent animal. I know *exactly* how you feel, but understand that *it was the only way*, and it *had* to be done!" (See Isaiah 53:4-6, Hebrews 9:11-14; 12:2)

When I say I heard God speak to me, it may sound far out to some. It was not an audible voice, but it was a voice that resonated in my spirit, clear and concise in a supernatural way. If you've ever experienced His voice, you have no doubt that it is God who is speaking.

Somehow I did understand. I knew for sure that an animal being sacrificed was not something God took pleasure in or even wanted to do, *but it was absolutely necessary for the future of His entire creation*. It was the only way to intervene in the catastrophe man had caused so long ago. That is, it was the only way until the time would come for the final and ultimate sacrifice of His own Son. (See Hebrews 7:27)

Hearing from God like I did that night stirred a desire deep inside for me to know and understand more about why the animals had to be sacrificed. Not only was I comforted by His words, but they also gave me the courage I needed to investigate further.

It was evident that it took a sacrifice to solve the dilemma that faced all of humanity. But what didn't make sense and seemed so unfair was that it had to involve the *innocent animals*. Why were they chosen to serve as part of the solution to a problem that was obviously caused by man? Why them? What possible benefit could they provide by giving up their lives; after all, shouldn't we be the ones? It seems only logical that if they had nothing to do with the mess man got into, why should they be expected to be a part of the solution?

Why on earth did God involve the innocent?

Not long after that experience, while I was studying it became obvious to me that there was something very significant about *why* God had chosen the animals for such an important role — *knowing it involved such horrific suffering on their part.*

As I continued on in my investigation, I began to discover some important truths relating to animals and their tremendous value to God, *and His Kingdom.* Today I realize that the subject of "Sacrifice" holds many vital keys where the animals are concerned. The meaning and purpose of a sacrifice soon became more important than I ever could have imagined.

When you understand the qualifications required for something to be eligible as a sacrifice, you will also understand — *why animals had to be placed in that position.*

WHAT I LEARNED

For something to be a sacrifice it must have great value!

The word "*sacrifice*" in *Webster's Dictionary* means: *To give up something valuable for the sake of another.*

The 1828 edition of *Webster's* says "sacrifice" means, "To make atonement for sin…"

The word "atonement" comes from an early Hebrew word, "Kaphar," and it means to *cover* sins. We'll see why that aspect is important as we continue.

In the eyes of God, a sacrifice had to be *worthy* and it had to meet certain *qualifications*.

The animals offered as sacrifices were loved and cherished

Under the Old Covenant, the Israelites lived in an *agrarian society* where they developed a bond with their animals. If a lamb was to be sacrificed, it had to be in *relationship* with both the man and his family. For us, it would be like offering one of our beloved pets as a sacrifice.

The Law required that they give up their most precious and perfect animal, and then personally witness it being brutally slaughtered for the sins *that they had committed*. It was truly a *sacrifice* for them.

Sacrifice — an innocent soul being laid down for a guilty one

In a sacrifice, the innocent one is a qualified substitute who pays the sin penalty so the guilty one can go free from sin. In the case of animal sacrifices, it was the animal who was required to give up their innocent life, so that a guilty man would be able to have a relationship with a Holy God.

The animal's blood was accepted because, unlike man's blood, it had not been tainted by sin. So when God looked at the person who offered the sacrifice, He no longer saw their sin because of the covering that had been provided by the blood of the innocent animal.

It was not that the blood covered the physical body of the man. That's not what happened. The blood covered his *sin*. It was a spiritual covering. Remember, man is a *spirit* and from the moment he is born, his *spirit* is disconnected from God — simply because of his *sin nature*. It was the innocent blood of a sacrificed animal that made it possible for a temporary reconnection of a man back to God.

In a sacrifice the innocent must die for the guilty!

There is no other way. Without the shedding of innocent blood, there can be no covering or atonement for sin.

The value of a sacrifice is priceless

We must not become desensitized to the impact that sacrifices had on all that were involved and the heartache they caused. God Himself, placed a high value on each and every one of them.

Because the animals served as a sacrifice for mans benefit, we might think more highly of ourselves than we should. Yes, it is true that it shows God's love for us, *but let's not depreciate the premium value due to the animals.* Jesus was also sacrificed and died for us, but that didn't place man in a higher position.

Because those innocent animals served in the way they did, they should be recognized, appreciated and honored. I did NOT say they should be *worshipped* — I said recognized, appreciated and honored. Jesus *alone* is worthy of worship! (See Romans 1:25)

The first sacrifice was performed by God

Out of God's great love and mercy for mankind, it became necessary for the *first* time to sacrifice one of His own beloved creatures because of the sin Adam committed in the garden of Eden. Had Adam not disobeyed God, there would never have been a need for animals to be sacrificed.

"...Behold, to obey is better than sacrifice..."
(1 Samuel 15:22 NKJV)

How must Adam have felt knowing he was the cause of their death? It must have been a horrible ordeal for everyone! Up until this time, no one had ever experienced death. Every one of those animals had been closer to Adam than we could ever imagine. They all lived together in a place that had never known sin. The relationships they had with one another were perfect in every way. Now Adam had to witness and experience death for the first time, *knowing that he was the one responsible.*

In addition to that, his own body immediately began the process of dying. It was not the physical death of his body that came about first, it was the death of his own spirit. (See the chapter, Free from Eternal Death.) The result was a total breakdown in fellowship with his eternal life source — *God*. Adam immediately knew what it was like to experience that hollow separation from God when his spirit died — an aloneness and an emptiness. It had been sin that caused his connection to be severed. *And it is sin that still causes man's separation from God.*

There would be no death for anyone— including the animals had there been no sin!

Animals were an acceptable sacrifice to God — proving they are innocent and sinless

If animals were not innocent, they would not qualify as an acceptable sacrifice. To be innocent means *not guilty of any sin*. The human race does not have the innocence of animals. And because animals are sinless, *God does not and will not hold them responsible for sin*. This means that they will not face the *judgment* that all sinners will one day have to face. (See Hebrews 9:27)

Why are animals sinless?

Animals were divinely positioned to be under man's authority. That means, *from the beginning* they were subjected to man's authority with absolutely no say in the matter.

The one who holds the position of authority over another is *the one* who is held responsible and accountable for those under him. Adam was *the one* given the command not to eat from the specific tree in the garden of Eden, and he was *the one* who disobeyed. The animals were not given this command; consequently, they never disobeyed or rebelled against God.

It was the man Adam, who had been placed in charge over the rest of creation for their protection and welfare.

It was the man who relinquished all he had been given to the enemy of God.

And it was the man who ranked highest in authority and surrendered it all in an act of disobedience *causing the entire fall.*

Man alone sinned, not the animals!

Another reason that animals are sinless is because Adam's blood does not run through their veins.

The *sin nature* is transferred through the blood of our *fathers* and can be traced all the way back to Adam. (See the chapter, God's Perfect Eternal Plan.) We are all descendants of Adam, therefore the *sin nature* comes through each one of us. With the exception of Adam, there has been only one *human being* ever to be born without a contaminated bloodline — Jesus, the Son of God.

Jesus is the only Man who ever lived a sinless life

Unlike man, animals have no sin running through their bloodline. This means sin is not passed on from one generation to the next. Consequently, animals remain sinless!

Sin affects our relationship with God

Remember, it is sin that disconnects man from God. Unlike man the animals are sinless, therefore their connection to God has never been broken. Before the fall, there was *communion* between man, the animals and God. It has always been the will of God for *all of creation* to be in communion with Him — as well as with one another.

We know that there was a divine order placed on creation from the beginning, and that it was mankind who held the leadership position with complete authority. (See Genesis 1:28.) However, that did not change God's desire or ability to commune with His *entire* creation. I find it amazing, that at one time it was the *blood of a sinless animal* that had qualified to *cover man's sin,* enabling him to be in communion with God. And so from the beginning, animals have played a vital role in reconnecting man back to God.

Where would we be if it weren't for the innocent?

The shedding of the blood of an innocent animal was necessary, but all it could do for many years was *cover* man's sin. Those sacrificed animals served as a *temporary bridge* connecting man back to God. They paid the price with their lives, until the time came nearly 2000 years ago when they no longer had to die on behalf of sinful humanity. God Himself knows only too well what it's like to have a loved one die a horrific death while serving mankind.

It was a sacrifice for God when He gave
His only begotten Son! (See John 3:16)

The ultimate sacrifice was finally made,
Once and for all —
through the blood of the Son of God Himself

Again, with an animal sacrifice sins could only be *covered*, but now, with Christ's sacrifice man's sin is *cleansed* and *forgiven* — *forever*. Forgiveness is available for all who *choose* to receive the sacrifice that Christ has made.

While the *covering* of sin was vitally important under the Old Covenant, it was still only a temporary solution. There is a huge difference between *covered* sin and *forgiven* sin!

The Ultimate Sacrifice

What it all comes down to is the fact that every human being is born with a sin nature and *we all need a Savior!*

Remember, the sin nature of man came through Adam and continues to flow through our fathers and down to us. It doesn't matter what kind of background you may have. Whether Hindu, Buddhist, Muslim, Catholic, Pentecostal, Baptist or any other religion, it does not matter — *we were all born in sin.* Even the innocent blood of bulls and goats could only cover, and not remove our sin. Their blood could not eternally save us. The sacrifice of an animal was only intended to keep man in relationship with God until our Savior, Jesus, made the ultimate and final sacrifice. When Jesus laid His life down, His blood went beyond merely covering our sins, to cleansing us and *setting us free from all sin.*

> To Him who loved us and *washed* us from our sins *in His own blood.*
> (Revelation 1:5 NKJV)

Every one of us is free to receive Jesus as our personal Savior and the forgiveness of our sin. God has left that decision up to us. But just like any other gift, it will never be ours until we *receive* it. When we do, we are not only cleansed from all sin, but we are *born again* from above. This single decision reconciles us back to God. Once we are reunited, we are also adopted as a child of God, and consequently we gain a loving heavenly Father for all of eternity.

Jesus is not ONE of the ways to get to God — He is the ONLY way!

Jesus said, "*I am the way, the truth, and the life. No one comes to the Father except through Me.*" (John 14:6 NKJV)

If you decide to reject the only acceptable payment provided by God, when your spirit leaves this earth you will have to pay for your sin yourself. *At that point, no one can help you and you cannot help yourself.* Sin must be paid for, and its wages are death.

> *For the wages of sin is death,*
> *but the gift of God is eternal life in Christ Jesus our Lord.*
> (Romans 6:23 NKJV)

Thankfully, the animals continue to be connected to God because of their innocence. Sin is not a factor in their lives. The acceptance of their blood as an innocent sacrifice under the Old Covenant proves this to be true.

It is by design that no animal carries even a trace of Adams guilty blood in their veins. And as a result, they have no sin to be cleansed or remitted. Because they have no sin to be forgiven, they have no sin debt to be paid. Animals, will never see hell because they are sinless. *Remember, there is no judgment or sentence of hell for the sinless.*

 Eternity with Your Pets

**If it were possible that animals could commit sin,
God would have made a way for their salvation —
the same as He did for man**

The fact that animals were an acceptable sacrifice, proves that they have a soul

The primary requirement for an acceptable sacrifice was the exchange of an innocent soul for a guilty soul — an innocent life for a guilty life — an innocent nephesh for a guilty nephesh. (The Hebrew word for soul is nephesh)

If an animal did not have a soul, then it would have only been an exchange of a body for a soul, instead of a soul for a soul. This means that in order for an animal to have been an acceptable sacrifice for man's sin — that animal would have had to have a soul!

And not only that, but the Bible also says that the life (soul) is in the blood

For the **life** (soul— nephesh) of the flesh is in the blood,
and I have given it to you upon the altar
to make atonement for your souls;
for it is the blood that makes atonement for the soul.
(Leviticus 17:11 — See also verse 14; and Genesis 9:4 NKJV)

If animals have blood, wouldn't they also have a soul?

It is important to remember that animal sacrifices are no longer necessary because the ultimate Sacrifice of God's Own Son was made on the cross — thereby fulfilling the law. (See Matthew 5:17)

Jesus abolished animal sacrificing!

The barbaric sacrifices that are taking place today with animals, children and other human beings — *are sacrifices that are being made to false gods.* They are DEMONIC!

BE AWARE: Even though animal sacrifices are no longer necessary or acceptable by God, there is coming a time in the very near future when they will be re-instituted for a period of time — 1150 days. (See Daniel 8:14 Complete Jewish Bible)

The Jews offered animals to be sacrificed up until the time that their Temple in Jerusalem was destroyed by the Roman army in AD 70. From that time until now, they have been unable to perform the ritual of animal sacrifices, simply because their Temple in Jerusalem no longer exists.

But that's about to change! Soon, and very soon, the Jewish people will be able to rebuild their Temple on the Temple Mount — referred to as The Third Temple. Construction will begin following the signing of the Peace Treaty. After the Temple is built, the Jews will once again resume the sacrificing of animals.

The <u>purpose</u> for these sacrifices is to cleanse the Temple according to the man-made laws of the Jews. These laws are not ordinances found in the Bible but rather are found in the writings of the ancient rabbinic Sanhedrin.

The Bible tells us that they will offer up sacrifices for a total of 2300 evenings and mornings — which would equate to 1150 days. (See Daniel 8:14 Complete Jewish Bible)

Again, the Jews who will be partaking in and performing the upcoming animal sacrifices, have been blinded to the Gospel and do not believe that Jesus Christ is the Lamb of God —- *the ultimate and final Sacrifice.* (See Romans 11:25 MEV) They believe in what they are doing, and that the true *Messiah* (Mashiach), will be revealed to them *after the Temple is restored to its rightful state.*

In the meantime, it is important for us to recognize that Bible prophecy is unfolding right before our eyes. We will continue to witness many historical events that will take place in Israel: such as the restoration of the Temple, the re-institution of animal sacrifices, the stopping of the sacrifices, and the revealing of the man of sin — the son of perdition. (See Daniel 9:27 and Daniel 11:31)

NO ONE will be able to stop these sacrifices for the duration of 2,300 evenings and mornings (1150 days). But at the completion of time, please be aware that it will be the *man of sin* (*Antichrist*) who will enter the temple and stop the sacrifices and offerings, *and set himself up declaring that he is God.* When this event takes place, it will bring about a time of great tribulation. (see Matthew 24:21)

> Do not let anyone *deceive* you in any way. For
> that Day will not come unless a falling away comes
> first, and the man of sin is revealed, the son of
> destruction, who opposes and exalts himself above
> all that is called God or is worshipped, *so that he
> sits as God in the temple of God, showing himself
> as God.* (2 Thessalonians 2:3-4 MEV)

I beseech all animal lovers — DO NOT BE DECEIVED BY THIS MAN — no matter how much you want to see an ending to the sacrificing of animals —

THIS MAN IS NOT A HERO, HE IS THE ANTI-CHRIST! DO NOT BE FOOLED — THIS MAN IS NOT GOD!

AN INNOCENT LIFE FOR A GUILTY LIFE!

As sacrifices, animals were a valuable and priceless part of God's creation. *God does not discard or annihilate what He considers to be valuable and priceless!*

The *finished work of the cross* ended the need for any animal to be sacrificed. Countless innocent animals were horrifically sacrificed *until the Savior rescued them by sacrificing Himself.* The ultimate sacrifice for all of creation was finally made *once and for all* through the shed blood of the Son of God Himself.

Not with the blood of goats and calves,
but with His own blood He entered the Most Holy Place
once for all, having obtained eternal redemption.
(Hebrews 9:12 NKJV)

This is the purpose of the life, death and resurrection of
Jesus Christ!

THANK GOD FOR THE INNOCENT!

9

9

More than Just a Body

When You send forth Your Spirit,
they are created...

(PSALM 104:30 MEV)

If there's more to you,
than what I see,
Will your eternity,
be with me?

Some say animals have no spirit, and some say they have no soul
But, what does the Bible say?

Whether an animal has a spirit or does not have a spirit is vital to what takes place once they die. If animals are in fact spirit beings, then they will live beyond the grave. Spirits never die — they are eternal!

But if animals are merely bodies made from dust, then life is over at the grave.

Your pets' *eternal destiny* has been *predetermined* by God, even before the foundation of the earth. As we investigate further, it will become obvious that there is something more to them than meets the eye. That something is the very essence of who they are — *spirit and soul.*

The objective of this chapter is to dispel the myths and false teachings concerning the fate of our pets; to show the importance of what it means to be a spirit and have a soul — but most of all, to allow the Bible to prove that animals are *more than just a body.*

There is an eternal part of animals, just as there is an eternal part of man

Have you ever been told that your pet won't go to heaven because they don't have a spirit? Maybe someone said it was because they don't have a soul. In both cases, *they* were wrong.

Let's begin by clarifying the fact that spirits are not souls, and souls are not spirits. Over the years religion has used spirit and soul as if they were the same, even interchangeable. Although they work in tandem, they are two very different entities.

The Bible makes a distinction between spirit and soul in the book of Hebrews. Listen to what it says:

> For the word of God is quick, and powerful,
> and sharper than any twoedged sword,
> piercing even to the dividing asunder of *soul and spirit,*
> and of the joints and marrow,
> and is a discerner of the thoughts and intents of the heart.
> (Hebrews 4:12 KJV)

The soul is *who* you are: your mind, your will and emotions. The spirit is the breath that gives life. Spirit is *what* you are. By design, spirit and soul are both *intangible* and immortal — *they will live on forever.* (Example: Luke 16:19-31)

**Without a spirit and without a soul,
animals would be lifeless lumps of clay,
void of thoughts and emotions — mere dummies**

Now, let's look at some examples of how people have been misled concerning the fate of their pets.

The first case scenario goes something like this:

"My dog Sandy just died. The whole family misses her terribly. The kids keep asking where she is, and they want to know if they'll ever see her again. Can you help me to know what to tell them?"

A typical answer… "I'm sorry to say, but when Sandy died that was the end for her. Animals are not made in the image of God. Only man was made in God's image and God is a spirit. *Because your dog was not made in God's image, she couldn't have a spirit. It's having a spirit that makes man different from the animals.* That's because it's the spirit that lives forever. I know you miss your dog, but when a pet dies — *it's over for them.* Their body simply goes back to dust."

Says who?

While that answer may sound somewhat convincing — *it is not true.* What we have here is an example of someone adding something to the Scripture to make it say what it doesn't. In this case, it comes from a misunderstanding of the following verses in Genesis.

Then God said, "Let us make man in our *image,* after our *likeness,* and let them have *dominion* over the fish of the sea, and over the birds of the air, and over the livestock, and over all the earth, and over every creeping thing that creeps on the earth."

So God created man in His own image;
in the image of God He created him;
male and female He created them.
(Genesis 1:26-27 MEV)

Now even though it is absolutely true that God is Spirit, (See John 4:24) and man is also spirit, nowhere in this passage does it say or imply that animals are not. In fact, nowhere in the Bible does it say or insinuate that animals are *just a body*.

When God said, "Let us make man in our image, after our likeness," He was referring to much more than the fact that man is a spirit. (See chapter God's Perfect Eternal Plan)

The *Strong's Exhaustive Concordance of the Bible* defines the original meaning of the word *image* to mean, "Illusion, resemblance; hence a *representative figure.*"

Webster's 1828 dictionary defines *representative* as: Bearing the character or power of another; as a council representative of the people.

A *representative* is therefore, someone who is chosen to act or speak on behalf of another.

If you read the entire first Chapter of Genesis, and keep it in proper context, you will see that the word "image" refers to man's *position*. That is to say, man was created to rule over creation in the same way that God would rule. He was placed and *positioned* here on earth to be God's *representative*.

In actual truth, what makes mankind different from the animals is not that he is a spirit being,
But that he was made in the image of God, after His likeness

It's foolish and vain for man to think that he alone was created to be the only eternal being. If that were the case, how would we ever explain the multitude of angels who are also spirit beings? They were not made in God's image, yet they are spirits and they are eternal. (See Hebrews 1:14, Psalm 104:4)

We know from the Bible that animals in Heaven are also spirit beings

Listed below are two accounts where horses come from Heaven to the earth for the purpose of aiding in battle. The first account has already taken place and involves the prophet Elisha and his servant.

The following is a summary of what took place as it was recorded in 2 Kings 6:15-17.

Elisha, and his servant awoke one morning and discovered that they were surrounded by a vast army with horses and chariots in what *appeared* to be an impossible situation. The servant said to Elisha, "Oh no, my master! What are we to do?" Elisha answered, "Do not be afraid, for those who are with us are more than those who are with them."

Then Elisha prayed and said, "Lord, please, *open his eyes* that he may see." And the Lord opened the servant's eyes and he saw; and behold, *the mountain was full of horses and chariots of fire surrounding Elisha.*

I mention this story about the invisible army of God because it includes a large number of horses — *horses, who are more than just a body.*

The second account is recorded in the book of Revelation and is still yet to come. When it does take place, **it will be the most glorious event that the world has ever seen!** It too, will involve horses who come from heaven to the earth for the purpose of assisting in battle.

This upcoming event that will soon *rock the world,* was revealed by God to the Apostle John through a vision. John describes how he saw heaven open and *Jesus descending to earth on a white horse. And not only did he see Jesus, but he also saw the armies of Heaven — all riding white horses. Horses who are more than just a body!*

NOTE: When Jesus came to earth the first time, He came to redeem all that was lost in the *fall*. But when Jesus returns for a second time, He will rule and reign as King of Kings and Lord of Lords!

> And I saw heaven opened, and behold a *white horse*;
> and he that sat upon him was called Faithful and True…
>
> And the armies which were in heaven followed him upon
> *white horses*, clothed in fine linen, white and clean.
> (Revelation 19:11, 14 KJV)

Based on the above eyewitness accounts, we know there are animals in heaven right now who are obviously spirit beings. Therefore, we have no reason to doubt that the ones here on earth are also spirit beings — *after all, the earth is a reflection of heaven.*

> Your kingdom come.
> Your will be done
> On earth as it is in heaven.
> (Matthew 6:10 NKJV)

There's another false belief that says,

"Animals can't go to heaven because they don't have a soul."

Says who?

This opinion is primarily based on a premise that says animals have no ability to think or reason; that they are only capable of acting out of instinct or in response to a certain stimuli. Basically, they are looked upon as being not much more than robots.

This is an erroneous teaching and anyone who believes it to be true must not have had any personal interaction with animals, *at least not with mine.* Those who spend some time with animals will tell you, this is complete and utter nonsense.

It is delusional and not at all what the Bible teaches or what the early church once believed. Yet, this falsehood has been passed down from one generation to the next, *as though it were the gospel.* As a matter of fact, I distinctly remember the first day of school when the professor of a major university posed this question to my animal science class, "How many of you believe that animals have the ability to think or reason?"

The overwhelming majority of the class answered with a resounding, "Yes." What happened next was a shock to us all. The instructor threatened to fail anyone in the class who would dare to disagree with the *philosophy* that states: *animals have no ability to think or reason, they act merely on instinct!*

My first thought was, *how will I ever pass this class?* Then in utter amazement I asked myself, *where does such ignorance come from?*

I subsequently discovered one source, and that was through a belief that was spearheaded and taught by the famous French philosopher, Rene Descartes. Many consider him to be the 'father of modern philosophy,' by his coining the phrase, "I think, therefore I am."

Descartes was popular during the seventeenth century "Enlightenment" period. And because of his influence, he managed to persuade others to believe in his unsubstantiated theory — *that animals have no soul.*

Unfortunately, this fallacy has continued to spread and is still prevalent, even today.

Descartes promoted and taught that animals were nothing more than *complex automata* — equivalent to robots. He practiced and advanced the horrific and cruel acts of *animal vivisection* because he believed they were *incapable of feeling pain.*

Descartes recognized that animals could see, hear and touch, but insisted that they were not conscious, able to suffer or have language. He concluded that *animals have no soul, mind or ability to reason.*

I'm sure that most of you would agree with me that Mr. Descartes must not have had a personal relationship with even one animal, to have ever believed or promoted such an ignorant philosophy.

The Bible has many examples that refute this teaching of Descartes.

For instance, the Book of Job tells us that animals are not only capable of thinking and reasoning, but that they also have a soul.

> "But now ask the beasts, and let them teach you:
> and the birds of the air, and let them tell you;
> or speak to the earth, let it teach you;
> and let the fish of the sea declare to you.
> Who among all these does not know
> that the hand of the Lord has done this,
> *in whose hand is the* **soul** *[Hebrew nephesh] of every living thing,*
> and the breath of all mankind."
> (Job 12:7-10 MEV)

Did you know —
that the very word "soul" comes from the Latin word anima,
which is where we get the word "animal"?

Next, we have an amazing story from the book of Numbers that talks about a donkey and a man named Balaam. Now this is not a parable, but an actual account that reveals important truths about animals and the spirit realm. It attests to the fact that animals have both a spirit and a soul, just the same as man.

In this story we find that Balaam's donkey not only had the ability to reason and count, but that she also demonstrated a high level of compassion. It was obvious that her mind was sharp and able to make quick, quality decisions, ones that ultimately protected the life of her owner — *even to the **detriment** of her own life.*

> Then the Lord **opened** the mouth of the donkey,
> and she said to Balaam, 'What have I done to you,
> that you have struck me these three times?
> (Numbers 22:28 NKJV)

We also find that she had the capacity to comprehend language, as was evidenced by the way she carried on a rational conversation with Balaam, *that is* once the Lord *allowed* her to speak.

(That word *opened* means to loosen in Hebrew. See Strong's #6605)

Based on what she said, there was no doubt that she understood exactly what had taken place. She even questioned her abusive master about why he beat her three times. His response was that he would have killed her if he had a sword. (See Numbers 22:29)

This man was *blind* to the fact that his donkey had just heroically saved his life, while risking her own. (See 2 Corinthians 4:4)

This story of Balaam's donkey is literally an *eye opening* event that demonstrates animals are intelligent, kindhearted and capable of displaying an enormous amount of compassion. It also proves that they have a remarkable commitment and allegiance toward their owners, even in the midst of adversity.

Anyone who reads this account would be hard pressed to deny that animals have a mind, as well as the necessary mental faculties that enable them to reason and communicate.

As for Descartes, who *hypothesized* that animals have no capacity to suffer — well, let's just say, the donkey disproved his philosophy when she questioned the man as to why he beat her.

Suffice it to say, this dedicated donkey possessed every characteristic of a soul. Characteristics that Descartes claimed were absent from all animals!

You cannot see or operate in the spirit realm unless you are a spirit being!

The account of Balaam's donkey not only substantiates that animals have a soul (mind, will, and emotions), but that they are also spirit beings. You might ask, "How is that?" Well, in order to operate in the spirit realm, *a spirit is required*. Remember, the Bible makes it clear that the donkey was able to function and see exactly what was taking place in the spirit realm. The Lord did not have to open her spiritual eyes because they were already open — that was not the case for Balaam. The Lord had to open his eyes in order for him to see *what the donkey saw all along*.

This event supports the fact that she *is* indeed a spirit being. I emphasize the word *is* because it is present tense and I want to make a point of saying, the *spirit* of Balaam's donkey *is still very much alive today*. Even though her physical body has returned to dust, her spirit is very much alive and well. At this moment she is back with her Creator, God— in heaven.

Again, if the donkey were *just a body*, or even just a body with a soul, but had no spirit, **she would never have been able to see or operate in the spirit realm.**

This account of Balaam and his donkey provides evidence of the truth that man and animals are both spirit beings — *spirit beings who live in a body*.

Side-note for the naysayers

I know there are some people who deny that it was the donkey who was doing the talking on her own behalf, and insist that it was God speaking through her as though she were some sort of puppet. The Bible doesn't say or even imply that.

If you read what was recorded in Numbers Chapter 22, it's quite obvious that *the donkey figured out on her own how to protect Balaam*. This is confirmed in verse 33, when the Angel of the Lord said,

> *"The donkey saw Me and turned aside from Me these three times. If she had not turned aside from Me, surely I would also have killed you by now, and let her live."* (NKJV)

No one told her what to do and no one told her what to say. The Lord didn't mimic His words through her mouth any more than He used her body as a puppet. The donkey acted out of what was in her *heart* and spoke exactly what was on her *mind!*

If you carefully read the story, you will find that the Lord did speak to the prophet Balaam, but it was through the *mouth of the Angel of the Lord* — NOT THE DONKEY!

To deny what happened is to deny the truth of the word of God.

Let me also clear up any confusion you may have from a corresponding verse in 2 Peter 2:16, that says, "...a *dumb donkey* speaking with a man's voice restrained the madness of the prophet." (NKJV)

When it refers to the donkey as being *dumb*, that simply means that she was mute and had been unable to speak. A *man's voice* is defined in this case to mean a human's voice.

The actions of Balaam's donkey proves that she is not only a spirit being but that she also has a soul!

If you have ever had a pet ask yourself the following questions:

Does your pet have: *dreams, memories, feelings, thoughts, emotions, free will or personality?*

Does your pet: *give or receive love?*

Have you ever had a special relationship with a pet?

If your answer is "yes" to any of the above, then your pet has a soul!

This is just as true for all of the so called *wild animals,* as it is for our domesticated pets. All animals have a soul!

Another example used to say that animals are "just a body," comes from the misuse of the following Scripture.

And the Lord God formed man of the dust of the ground,
and breathed into his nostrils the *breath of life*;
and man became a living soul.
(Genesis 2:7 KJV)

This verse says nothing about the creation of women or the creation of animals. However, this verse is often quoted regarding the creation events for both of them.

The fact that both women and animals have the *breath of life* residing in them is evident; otherwise, they would be without life. It is only logical to conclude that both women and animals have a soul, regardless of how or when God breathed the breath of life into them. Just because the Bible does not provide an account of this part of God's work, does not mean that it did not happen.

Animals would not be alive
without the breath of life

If this verse was intended to mean that animals are not eternal beings, then women are in trouble as well. The Bible does not say that God breathed the breath of life into Eve's nostrils. But, the Bible does say the following about the creation of Eve:

Then the rib which the Lord God had taken from man He
made into a woman, and He brought her to the man.
(Genesis 2:22 NKJV)

That word *made* can also be translated as *built*. But again, there is no mention of God breathing the breath of life into the woman's nostrils.

Does that verse mean that men have souls, but women and animals do not? Of course not.

The Bible may not specifically say that God breathed into the nostrils of the woman or the animals, but it also doesn't say that He didn't.

However, the Bible does say in Psalm 104:30 that God sent forth His Spirit and they were created.

The Bible also says that all flesh has been given the breath of the spirit of life.

> And all flesh died that moved on the earth: birds and cattle and
> beasts and every creeping thing that creeps on the earth, and
> every man. *All in whose nostrils was the breath of the spirit of life,*
> all that was on the dry land, died. (Genesis 7:21- 22)

Whole doctrines have been built around that verse (Genesis 2:7), where people have concluded that animals have no soul, even though there are many other verses that refer to the breath, life and soul of an animal. The truth is, the Bible makes many references to both mankind and animals as having a soul.

And finally, let us look at the last example they use to say that animals are "just a body."

They say, "The Bible says in Ecclesiastes that when an animal dies they go down into the ground and that's the end of them. And because they are *just a body* they turn back to dust and are simply annihilated."

Says who?

> Then I thought in my heart: Regarding the account of sons of men,
> God is making clear to them to show that they are but animals.
> For what befalls the sons of men befalls animals; as one dies,
> so dies the other. ***There is one breath for all of them;***
> there is no advantage for man any more than animals, for all is vanity.
> All go to one place: All are from the dust and all return to dust.
> *Who knows whether the spirit of man goes upward and the **spirit**
> **of animals** goes down to the earth?*
> (Ecclesiastes 3:18-21 MEV)

Anyone who jumps to the conclusion that when an animal dies it goes into the earth, but when a person dies they go to heaven, has missed the objective of this verse. That may appear to be what was said if you're a casual reader. But, *if you carefully read what was written,* you'll recognize that Solomon was asking a question. He was *not* making a doctrinal statement that says when an animal dies he lays in the earth, and when man dies he goes to heaven.

With a close examination of this passage, the question that's being asked is, "**Who knows** whether the *spirit* of man goes upward, and whether the *spirit* of the animal goes downward **to** the earth?" (See Ecclesiastes 3:21)

Solomon was not saying that an animal's life ends in the grave. What he said was their bodies are made of dust and their bodies will turn back to dust, the same as man. They both return to the same place.

> The dust returns to the earth where it was,
> *And the spirit returns to God who gave it.*
> (Ecclesiastes 12:7 MEV)

So, a more relevant question to ask would be, *do other beings have a spirit and if so, are they going to heaven?* For the answer, let's take a look at the rest of what Solomon had to say.

First of all, he made it clear that this one thing will happen to both man and animals alike, "as one dies, so dies the other." Then he made a point of saying, "There is one breath for all of them;" (See Ecclesiastes 3:19, above)

That word *breath* in the *Strong's,* is the Hebrew word *ruwach* (spirit). It is the same word used in Ecclesiastes 12:7. "And the *spirit* (ruwach) returns to God who gave it."

Young's Literal Translation has the following to say regarding verse 19:

> For an event [is to] the sons of man, and an event [is to] the beasts,
> even one event [is] to them; as the death of this, so [is] the death
> of that; and *one spirit* [is] to all, and the advantage of man
> above the beast is nothing, for the whole [is] vanity.
> (Ecclesiastes 3:19 YLT)

Another important point that Solomon emphasized was the fact that man has *no preeminence* above an animal. The King James translation says it this way, "...yea, they have all one breath; so that a man hath no *preeminence* above a beast: for all is vanity."

Notice that he did not say that animals have no *preeminence* above man. The context of preeminence was *not* referring to the *dominion* that man had initially been given over the animals, but about the death of both man and animals.

In the *Strong's Concordance*, **PREEMINENCE** means, gain or superiority. In other words, man has no superiority or gain over the animals when it comes to dying. This refers to the spirit part of an animal as well as the physical body. Remember, he told us in Ecclesiastes 3:19, above,

> "Surely, they have all *one breath* (spirit)…"

Now according to what Solomon has said, and what modern science confirms, the physical body of both man and animals are made from dust and will turn back to dust. That is not what happens to the spirit and soul. They are both intangible, *indestructible* and eternal. They come from God and will return to God, the only One who can give life. (See Ecclesiastes 12:7 above)

We also know that at the point of death there is a separation of the spirit and soul from the body. This is true for both man and animals alike.

When the spirit leaves, the body dies because it is the spirit that gives life to the body. Spirits are eternal; they never die!

James 2:26, says, *"For as the body without the spirit is dead…"*

That brings us to Ecclesiastes 3, verse 21, where Solomon raises a very important question. "Who knows the *spirit of the sons of men,* which goes upward, and the *spirit of the animal,* which goes down to the earth?"
(Ecclesiastes 3:21 NKJV)

It's important because within the question itself, he specifically states that there is a spirit component to animals, just the same as there is a spirit component to man.

That answers the all-important question — *Yes, animals have a spirit*!

So, don't be discouraged or confused by what *they say.*

Let the word of God be your final authority.
Your pet is spirit and soul with eternal destiny.

ANIMALS ARE — MORE THAN JUST A BODY!

The following Scriptures support the fact that animals do indeed have a soul —

Genesis 1:20, And God said, "Let the waters bring forth abundantly the moving creature that hath *life* (Hebrew "soul"), and fowl that may fly above the earth in the open firmament of heaven." (KJV)

Important Note: Older King James Bibles show in the footnote that the Hebrew word for *"life"* is *soul.* Somehow this was left out of some modern translations.

Genesis 1:21, And God created great whales, and every *living creature* (soul*)* that moveth, which the waters brought forth abundantly, after their kind, and every winged fowl after his kind: and God saw that it was good. (KJV)

Note: The Hebrew word for "creature" is *nephesh* and it means *soul.* (Strong's Concordance #5315)

Genesis 1:24, And God said, "Let the earth bring forth the living *creature* after his kind, cattle, and creeping thing, and beast of the earth after his kind: and it was so." (KJV)

Genesis 1:30, "To every beast of the earth and to every bird of the air and to everything that creeps on the earth which has the breath of life (a living soul) in it, I have given every green plant for food." And it was so. (MEV)

IMPORTANT NOTE: The older King James Bible shows us in the footnote that the word "life" in the Hebrew means "a living soul." Newer translations have left this marginal reading out.

To further validate that an animal is a living soul, let us take a look at Genesis 2:7. In this verse we find the exact same Hebrew word being used to describe man as "a living soul" that was used earlier in Genesis 1:30, to describe the animals as "a living soul"

Genesis 2:7, And the Lord God formed man of the dust of the ground, and breathed into his nostrils the breath of life; and man became *a living soul.* (KJV) (Strong's #2416)

Genesis 2:19, And out of the ground the Lord God formed every beast of the field, and every fowl of the air; and brought them unto Adam to see what he would call them: and whatsoever Adam called *every living creature* (soul -nephesh Strong's #5315), that was the name thereof. (KJV)

Genesis 9:9-10, "And I, behold, I establish my covenant with you, and with your seed after you; And with every *living creature* (soul-nephesh) that is with you, of the fowl, of the cattle, and of every beast of the earth with you; from all that go out of the ark, to every beast of the earth." (KJV)

Genesis 9:12, And God said, "This is the token of the covenant which I make between me and you and every *living creature* (soul - nephesh) that is with you, for perpetual generations:" (KJV)

Genesis 9:15, "And I will remember my covenant, which is between me and you and every *living creature* (soul - nephesh) of all flesh; and the waters shall no more become a flood to destroy all flesh." (KJV)

Genesis 9:16, "And the bow shall be in the cloud; and I will look upon it, that I may remember the everlasting covenant between God and every *living creature* (soul - nephesh) of all flesh that is upon the earth." (KJV)

Now let's take a look at a few more Scriptures in the Book of Leviticus that also confirm that animals have a soul.

Leviticus 11:46, This is the law of the beasts, and of the fowl, and of every *living creature* (chay nephesh) that moveth in the waters, and of every creature (soul - nephesh) that creepeth upon the earth: (KJV)

Leviticus 24:17-18, And he that killeth any *man* shall surely be put to death. And he that killeth a *beast* shall make it good; beast for beast. (KJV)

IMPORTANT NOTE: The same Hebrew word for soul (nephesh) is applied to both man and animals in verses 17 and 18.

Other Scriptures of the Bible that also confirm that animals have a soul.

Proverbs 12:10, A righteous man regardth the **life** (soul - nephesh) of his beast: but the tender mercies of the wicked are cruel. (KJV)

Numbers 31:28, And levy a tribute unto the Lord of the men of war which went out to battle: **one soul** (nephesh) of five hundred, *both of the persons, and of the beeves* (cows)*, and of the asses, and of the sheep:* (KJV)

Note: The word "soul" (nephesh) above refers to "persons," "beeves," "asses" and "sheep."

Job 12:7-10, "But ask now the beasts, and they shall teach thee; and the fowls of the air, and they shall tell thee: Or speak to the earth, and it shall teach thee: and the fishes of the sea shall declare unto thee. Who knoweth not in all these that the hand of the Lord hath wrought this? In Whose hand is the *soul* (nephesh) of every living thing, and the breath of all mankind." (KJV)

Psalm 74:19, "O deliver not the *soul* (nephesh #5315) of thy turtledove unto the multitude of the wicked: forget not the congregation of thy poor for ever." (KJV)

Revelation 16:3, And the second angel poured out his vial upon the sea; and it became as the blood of a dead man: and every *living soul* (psuche) died in the sea. (KJV)

Note: The New Testament Scriptures original language is in the Greek, and it also describes animals as having a soul. Some newer translations have changed the word to say, "creature" or "thing."

Under the **Old Covenant** the word "soul" is translated from the Hebrew word *nephesh* and in the New Covenant it's translated from the Greek word *psuche*.

THE BIBLE LEAVES NO DOUBT THAT BOTH MAN AND
ANIMALS HAVE A LIVING SOUL.

10

The Promise of the Resurrection

...the creature itself also shall be delivered from the bondage of corruption into the glorious liberty of the children of God.

(ROMANS 8:21 KJV)

Did you know, that after your pet passes there will come a time when they will return to the earth to live forever in a *glorified body*? A *glorified body* is one that's perfected and free from the effects of sin; it's *incorruptible* and immortal.

There will come a moment, in the twinkling of an eye, when the bodies of our pets will be resurrected. To be *resurrected* means that God will raise their bodies up from the grave and then restore them to a glorified condition.

That's right! Your pets us will get back the same body they had when they lived with you here on earth, only this time it will be perfect — *because this time it will be glorified.*

In other words, *the resurrection of your pet's body will be the transformation of the same body they had while living here on earth.*

Your pets will live in a glorified body throughout eternity

So, how do we know that the bodies of our pets will be resurrected?

The next few verses of scripture give us the answer, but the fullness of their truth has not always been recognized. That being the case, let us pay close attention and allow the scripture to illuminate the following truth: *the resurrection of an animal's body is connected to the resurrection of the children of God.*

Animals know they have an eternal future!

The Bible says;

> For the earnest expectation of the creature waiteth for the manifestation of the sons of God.
>
> For the creature was made subject to vanity, not willingly, but by reason of him who hath subjected the same in *hope,* Because the creature itself **also shall be delivered** from the *bondage of corruption* into the glorious liberty of the children of God.
>
> For we know that the whole creation groaneth and travaileth in pain together until now.
>
> **And not only they, but ourselves also,** which have the firstfruits of the Spirit, **even we ourselves** groan within ourselves, **waiting for the adoption,** to wit, **the redemption of our body**. (Romans 8:19-23 KJV)

First, we must establish who it is that the Apostle Paul is referring to as *the creature* in verses 19-21.

In the original Greek language the word is ktisis and translated to mean, *creation, creature, created thing.* With that understanding and based on the word of God, we can eliminate the following:

- God's angels — because they are not in a fallen state and do not need *deliverance."*
- Fallen angels — because they have an eternal destiny in the lake of fire.
- Non believers — because the Bible tells us that they are eternally lost and without hope.
- Born again believers — because verse 23 is referring to them when it says; "And not only they, but ourselves also…"

Therefore, it should be obvious that Romans 8:19-21 is referring to the *animals*!

NOTICE: The author of Romans, the Apostle Paul, would not have said in verse 23, *"ourselves also…even we ourselves…"* unless the reference included others.

So, who else besides the *children of God* does this verse include?

Again, it includes the animals.

The above portion of scripture indicates that animals know *exactly* what the future holds. We know this to be true, because in the original Greek it tells us that they are not only waiting, but *anxiously* waiting and *watching* with *intense anticipation* — proving that animals have cognitive ability. (King James says, earnest expectation.)

What are the animals waiting for?

They are groaning and crying out in expectation because they are waiting for the revealing of the sons of God.

Why are the animals waiting?

Because they have *no* other option. The animals were *made to submit* to the vanity (wickedness) of man; and because of their subordinate position they must wait for the Day of Redemption. On that day *they will be fully delivered, along with the sons of God.*

Also, the above portion of scripture tells us that the animals are *eagerly* waiting with *persistent expectation*. And if they are expecting, that means they must know something.

What do the animals know?

The answer to this is key. The animals know and understand that their deliverance from the bondage of corruption and the resurrection of their bodies is *directly connected to the completed redemption of mankind.* The Bible says when man *shall be delivered*, creation will be delivered as well, as indicated by the use of the word *also.*

Animals are conscience of the fact that they have an eternal future connected to the children of God.

Why are the creatures groaning and travailing in pain, along with the children of God?

Because they, too, are waiting for the complete recovery of their bodies from death and corruption — in other words, the redemption of their bodies.

(REDEEM means to purchase back, to ransom, to liberate or rescue from captivity or bondage — to recover.)

Even though Jesus Christ regained every single thing that was lost in the *fall*, the *children of God* have only received a part of their possession.

Note: It is imperative to understand that even though we are all God's creation, **we are not all the children of God.** As a matter of fact, *no one is born into this world as a child of God.* This is because we are *all* born with the tainted blood of Adam that comes through our natural father's bloodline. Scripture tells us that Satan is our father at birth because of the inherited sin. (See John 8:44, 1 John 3:8-10, John 1:12))

The fact of the matter is, we all have the opportunity to become a child of God, but the truth is, most people don't know what is required. The answer is really quite simple. In order *for anyone to become a child of God, we must be adopted.* The qualification for adoption is that we put our faith in Jesus Christ.

> *For ye are all the children of God by faith in Christ Jesus.*
> (Galatians 3:26 KJV)

The Children of God know they have an inheritance

The following verse tells us *exactly* what *God's children* are waiting for in order to obtain their complete inheritance.

...even we ourselves groan within ourselves,
waiting for the adoption, *to wit* (that is to say), **the redemption of our body.**
(Romans 8:23 KJV)

In other words, the children of God are waiting for the fulfillment of the process which the adoption into the family of God guarantees; that is, the glorification of their physical bodies which will take place at The Resurrection.

So for the child of God, the redemption of their body will be the completion of their adoption. (See verse 23 above) The Bible refers to this as the *Day of Redemption.* (See Ephesians 4:30)

Therefore, the redemption of man is not complete until the whole man is redeemed: spirit, soul and body. But, as for the complete redemption of the animals, *the only requirement is the redemption of their bodies.*

Salvation is complete when the physical body is set free — Free from dust and death, to glory and immortality

Note: The resurrection of the animals is linked to the *redeemed* and *not the lost.* However, those of mankind who are *lost and without hope* will still be resurrected and stand before the *great white throne judgment.*

...there will be a resurrection of the dead,
both of the just and the unjust.
(Acts 24:15 NKJV)

What else can we learn from the above portion of scripture concerning the animals' present and future condition?

We learn that the animals have no choice in the matter, and therefore they have become slaves under the corruption of this world system.

"For the creature was made subject to vanity, not willingly, but by reason of *him* who hath subjected the same in *hope,*" (Romans 8:20 KJV)

The word, *him*, in the above verse is referring to God. And while it may be hard for some to understand *why* God would subject the animals to *depravity*, the Scripture tells us that *He had a reason. I believe* the reason goes all the way back to Genesis, when God laid out the divine order for creation.

In the beginning, God placed the animals under man's authority *for a reason. That reason was for their protection and welfare.* (See Genesis 1:28)

However, when man fell and sin entered the picture, divine order turned into chaos and the protection for the animals was no longer in place. As a result, they instantly became subject to vanity (evil) and to the moral corruption of man.

So, without a doubt the animals have been *made* to suffer the consequences of man's fall. And not only the animals, but the entire creation has been subjected to man's sinfulness. BUT even so, *God has given the animals hope for a future* with the *expectation* that they *will be delivered* and freed from the slavery of ruin, along with the children of God.

> "…but by reason of him who hath subjected the same in *hope,*"
> (Romans 8:20 KJV)

What is hope?

Strong's Concordance says that **HOPE** is "*an expectation of what is sure* (certain)" #1680. This kind of *hope* is not natural, it is divine.

This *hope* comes from God, and is not just an optimistic outlook or wishful thinking on something that has no substance to it, but rather it is a *confident expectation* based on a solid certainty.

Biblical hope rests on God's promises, with an expectation that He will not fail. This hope knows that whatever God has said, *will surely come to pass. It is certain because it is divinely guaranteed!* (See Joshua 23:14 KJV)

Romans 8:20 tells us the hope that animals have, comes from God. They understand that they cannot reverse their post-fall condition on their own. This means that their hope is not *founded on their own abilities,* but in the assurance of knowing that God *cannot* fail. This is why the creatures wait with *intense anticipation* for the fulfillment of His promise, *because they know —*

> God is not a man, that He should lie,
> nor a son of man, that He should repent.
> Has He spoken, and will He not do it?
> Or has He spoken, and will He not make it good?
> (Numbers 23:19 MEV)

And so, God's promise to creation is:

> "...*the creature itself also shall be delivered from*
> *the bondage of corruption into the glorious liberty of*
> *the children of God...*"
> (Romans 8:21 KJV)

Deliverance — not destruction!

Let me point out something that should be obvious, but for some reason has often gone unnoticed. The above verse plainly states that the animals *will be delivered* from the curse, yet there are those who say animals are destroyed or annihilated when they die. *It can't be both ways!* Either what the Bible says is true, and the animals *are delivered from the curse,* or the Bible is wrong and they are destroyed.

If the animals that God put here on earth
were destroyed or ceased to be,
that would mean they were never actually delivered!
It would also mean that their hope was in vain.
But, that is not the case because the Bible plainly states —
The creature itself also shall be delivered!

Again, the *hope* that God has given to every animal is that they will participate in the freedom of the glory of the children of God. And that they too will be delivered from the bondage of decay.

Note: Luke 3:4-6, tells us that *all flesh* shall see the salvation of God.

In the meantime, all of creation is suffering. The earth is coming apart. The entire creation is groaning and travailing with birth pains; pains that are rapidly increasing. *Oddly enough, the animals are the ones who have the ability to forecast disasters.*

There are daily reports of earthquakes, tsunamis, floods, droughts, tornadoes, volcanoes, fires and hurricanes. Scientists say it's because of the environment, but the Bible says *its because of sin!* According to the Scriptures, there is a direct correlation between sin and the land.

Also, the Bible does warn us that a **real global warming** is indeed coming— it will occur when God Himself will purify the earth by fire. In Noah's day, the first purging of the earth was with water. After the second purging with fire, there will be a *renewed* earth — despite these events, *the earth will remain!*

The fact that all of these things are occurring more frequently is further proof that the Word of God is true.

Why will the earth be renewed?

Then He who sat on the throne said,
"Behold, I make all things new."
(Revelation 21:5 NKJV)

Heaven is a very real place! Heaven is where the redeemed along with the animals, join in worship as well as a multitude of other festivities. But most of all, Heaven is where the Lord Jesus Christ and His Father, God Almighty reside.

Now as magnificent as heaven is, this *present heaven* is not the final destination for the redeemed or the animals. And what most people don't realize is; those who are redeemed will be coming back to the New Earth along with the animals — not floating around on a cloud somewhere, playing a harp. The truth is, *we were all made and fashioned with a physical body and created to live here on this earth.*

However, there has been a misunderstanding among some that the heavens and the earth will be completely annihilated in the end, and that God will make *new heavens* and a *new earth*.

This confusion comes from a misunderstanding of 2 Peter 3:12-13 which says;

"*...because of which the heavens will be dissolved, being on fire, and the elements will melt with fervent heat? Nevertheless we, according to His promise, look for new heavens and a new earth in which righteousness dwells*", and also Revelation 21:1 that says; "*Now I saw a new heaven and a new earth, for the first heaven and the first earth had passed away...*"

At first, it may appear that those two verses contradict what I am saying about the earth being renewed and not destroyed, *but they don't.* The Bible never contradicts itself, and once you understand the meaning of the word *new* in the original Greek language, it will become clear that the earth will indeed be *renewed,* and not destroyed.

We find that there are two words in the original Greek language that are used to describe something as *new.* The first word is *neo,* which describes something that is *new in time* — such as a house that was just built. But if we are talking about a house that is *newly restored to its original condition,* a different word is used in the Greek — *kainos.*

Kainos also means new, but it is describing something that is *qualitatively new or renewed.* Once something is old (archaios) such as a restored house, it can no longer be described as *neo,* but instead it must be referred to as *kainos*

Kainos is the word used to describe "new" in both 2 Peter 3:12-13 and Revelation 21:1 — not *neo.* In other words, both of those passages use the word *kainos,* which clearly indicates that the heavens and the earth will be *renewed* — not destroyed and replaced. *Both verses are saying that the current heaven and earth will pass from one condition to another.*

So, what actually happens is that the earth will go through a *cleansing and purging process by fire.* But following that, God will redeem the earth and restore it — NOT ANNIHILATE IT — and then, the *renewed earth* will be inhabited by the redeemed along with the animals.

Therefore, the *final destination* for the animals and God's people is *not going up to God in heaven* while the earth is being destroyed. But rather, the final destination will be living on the renewed earth, and God will come down to dwell among His people and His creation — *which includes the animals.*

Note: Because the redemption of the earth is also linked to the redemption of man, the earth cannot be restored until after the great white throne judgment and the completed redemption of humanity.

The question is not whether animals will be on the New Earth, but rather, will our pets also be on the New Earth.

Another fallacy concerning the animals is the false teaching that says Romans 8 is referring only to a "new batch" of animals that would come to the earth *after the earth is restored.* If this were true, it would mean that Romans 8 does not apply to any animal who lived *prior* to the New Earth.

Again, those who take this stand are not denying that there will be animals living among the redeemed on the New Earth, but what they are denying is the fact that *those animals who have suffered through the bondage of corruption will also be included in God's plan of redemption.*

They mock and reject the notion of any past or present animal being a part of the resurrection.

Is it not just, that those animals who undeservingly suffered and cried out for relief on the old cursed earth, would be the same animals allowed to enjoy peace on the new earth?

 Eternity with Your Pets

As would be expected, those same people who deny that our pets will be on the New Earth are the very same ones who ridicule anyone who believes that animals have a spirit or a soul. And many times they become angry and hostile whenever the subject is brought up concerning animals and eternity.

They adamantly oppose the idea of any animal being redeemed or resurrected, and criticize anyone who has the hope of their pets joining them on the New Earth — *without any basis of support from the Scripture!*

When defending their position, some of them say it's what they were taught to believe, and others say it's what their parents told them — *regrettably, some are prominent ministers of the gospel.* The Bible tells us the traditions of men make the word of God of no effect.

What they are doing is passing down something they've always heard and accepting it as truth, instead of finding out what the Bible actually says. Whatever happened to "rightly dividing the word of truth?" (See 2 Timothy 2:15)

That being said, their arguments are altogether contrary to what Romans 8 is conveying, *as it pertains to the animals.*

God's **perfect eternal plan** *is to redeem the* **ENTIRE** *creation from the* **EFFECTS** *of sin. In other words, everything God created is eternal!*

Man is eternal, the earth is eternal, the heavens are eternal, angels are eternal *and the animals are eternal.*

The *renewed earth* will be filled with *renewed people* and *renewed animals.* God doesn't have to discard the animals He has already created and start over again. God is a God of restoration — not re-creation. Jesus Christ paid the price for restoration for *all of creation!*

Jesus said, "Behold, I am making all things new." (kainos)
(Revelation 21:5 ESV)

DANGEROUS MISCONCEPTIONS ABOUT LIFE AFTER DEATH!

Body sleep — not soul-sleep

Soul-sleep is the teaching that says when a person dies, his soul "sleeps" in his body until the time of the final resurrection and judgment of God. In other words, when the body is put into the ground, so is the soul.

My first question would be: "If a body is burned up, blown up or disintegrated, then where does the soul go if it's supposed to be asleep in the body?"

TAKE HEED: The term "soul-sleep" is not a Scriptural term. The Bible does not teach the doctrine of soul-sleep!

When the Bible uses the word "sleep," it is simply another term for *physical death* because the body *appears* to be asleep. *Never* does it apply to the spirit or the soul because they continue to exist after death — *they are immortal*.

An in-depth study shows that the metaphor of *sleep* refers to the physical body's inanimate state after death — *not the soul's*. In actual fact, you will never find the soul linked to sleep anywhere in the Bible. This is because it is only the body that *sleeps* and goes back to dust. Simply put, the body is referred to as *sleeping* until it is raised up in the resurrection.

We find in the Scriptures, that Jesus Himself always referred to physical death as *sleep*. For example, when Lazarus died, He told His disciples, "Our friend Lazarus *sleeps,* but I go that I may wake him up." (John 11:11 NKJV)

Romans 8:23 tells us that it is the *body* that waits to be redeemed — not the spirit or soul!

James 2:26 says, *"For as the body without the spirit is dead..."*

Sleep is clearly the biblical term for physical death

The Bible also teaches, that there is consciousness in the afterlife and that every human soul goes either to Heaven or to Hell the instant it leaves the body. For those who choose heaven, 2 Corinthians 5:8 says, *"We are*

confident, I say, and willing rather to be absent from the body, and to be present with the Lord." (KJV)

Now as it pertains to the animals, we know that they also have a soul, so when their body dies where does their soul go?

Contrary to what some believe, the soul of an animal does not go into the grave and sleep, any more than a human soul. Again, *souls do not sleep!*

There is no biblical basis for an animal's soul to go down into the bowels of the earth — nowhere in the Bible does it say that animals go to hell.

So, where does the soul of an animal go?

Answer: Back to the One who created them, the One who loves them the most and the One who owns them. Back to God Almighty — *El Shaddai*. (See Psalm 50:10)

The Bible is clear, when an animal or a person dies, the only part of them that goes into the ground is the body, an empty shell that *sleeps* until the time of the resurrection.

What needs to be put to death and utterly annihilated is the false doctrine of soul-sleep!

There is no such place as *Purgatory*

One of the most damnable doctrines is the one that teaches there is a holding tank (an intermediate place) located somewhere between heaven and hell. The truth is, there is no such place called **Purgatory** where a soul can go **after death** to be cleansed from the sins that were not satisfied during this life. Absolutely not! This is totally and completely unscriptural.

Jesus died to pay the penalty for all of our sins.
(See Romans 5:8 & Isaiah 53:5)

The idea of Purgatory is based on a misunderstanding of what Jesus Christ did on the cross at Calvary. For someone to say that we must also suffer in a place called Purgatory for our sins, is to say that the suffering Jesus endured was not enough.

To say that we must atone for our sins by cleansing in Purgatory is to say that the atoning sacrifice of Jesus Christ was insufficient. (See 1 John 2:2)

It is a complete failure not to recognize that Jesus' death was sufficient to pay the penalty for *all of our sins.*

The confusion comes when someone doesn't understand that they must *receive* the payment that was made on their behalf *before they die — not after they die.*

There is absolutely no further opportunity to repent of our sins, once our human spirit has departed from our body!

Do not be deceived and buy into the lie that says Purgatory is a *gift* from God that grants those who have died "in God's grace and friendship" an opportunity to undergo a purification process through fire and torment in a place called Purgatory, where they eventually become holy enough to get into heaven. *That will never happen!*

It's only through the shed blood of Jesus Christ that anyone can be cleansed, purified and reconciled to God. And without accepting Jesus Christ as your personal Savior along with what He did on the cross at Calvary, you will never see heaven — *or your pets!*

Please Note: 1 Corinthians 3:15 is in reference to the Judgment Seat of Christ — not an alleged Purgatory. It refers to a person's **WORK** being burned — not the **PERSON** being burned. Paul says *four* times that it is man's work that is being tested. (See 1 Corinthians 3:13-15)

What gets burned up is man's work that was done outside of Jesus Christ.

Although there is no such thing as a place of Limbo or Purgatory, there is a very real place called Hell — and it's far worse than anyone could ever imagine.

Hell is not only a total disconnect from God— but Hell is also the total absence of all animals!

In my opinion, many people who have died believing in a Purgatory are actually waiting in hell *thinking that they are in the purifying process of Purgatory.*

Is it possible that because of what they've been taught that they are hoping someone will either pray or buy them out from where they are? *It's sad to say — that will never happen.*

In truth, what these people are waiting for is actually the *great white throne judgment.* Whether they realize it or not, when they chose to believe in a place called Purgatory thinking it would cleanse them of their sins, they were rejecting Jesus Christ and the payment He made for them on the cross at Calvary.

You can't have it both ways; either choose the lie — Purgatory, or choose the truth — Jesus Christ and the atonement that He provided!

What about reincarnation?

I was in the barn working one day when an elderly neighbor paid me an unexpected visit. Mr. Spokes was a gentleman farmer who had been on a life-long quest to discover — *what happens after this life.* He was always dignified and reserved, but on this particular day he was beside himself.

Mr Spokes couldn't wait to tell me that he had finally found "the answer." He had just returned home from a visit with his daughter and could barely contain himself.

"Caren, I know the answer. It's the only thing that makes sense!" At first, I had no idea what he was talking about. I thought, "The answer to what?"

He went on to explain, "It's **reincarnation**! That's the only thing that makes any sense. When we die, our soul will be "reborn" into another body. What we come back as depends on *karma* — that is, the accumulation of everything we've ever done, both good and bad in this life and all of our other lives."

If only I had known the truth back then and conveyed it to Mr Spokes... what a difference it might have made in his eternal destiny.

Please be aware: The devil is a master at twisting words and perverting the truth and he has done exactly that with the biblical expression, *born again.* (See chapter "Free from Eternal Death," to learn what it really means to be born again.)

When an animal dies, they don't lie in the ground and soul-sleep any more than man does. They are not annihilated. They do not turn into nothingness. They are not out there floating around in cyberspace somewhere. And they are *definitely not* coming back to visit you in some other form — *as in another animal.* **NO!** *The soul of your pet is not reborn into another body, plant or divine being.*

Never buy into the lie that your pet who may have already passed on, is now in the body of a new pet or *whatever.* I know there are some who wish that this could be true, but…NO! NO! NO! A thousand times, NO! Not now — not ever!

It doesn't matter how much resemblance you think your pet's personality has to a prior pet, or how *coincidental* the circumstances may seem to be, *that is not what happens!*

Your dog does not become an angel, a reincarnated person or an animal watching over you!

What God has planned for you and your pets is infinitely better than anything you could ever imagine. If you only knew what it is like for your departed pet right now, you would *never* want them to come back to the earth in its present condition. And to be quite honest, no matter how much they still love you, they would not want to leave where they are — *even to be with you.* They are finally *free from the effects of sin and in the presence of God.*

Every single pet is unique and one of a kind, just like we are. Understand, your pets will not come back to this sin-filled earth in another body. However, the Bible does say that once your pet passes, there is coming a time when the *very same body* their soul once occupied will be resurrected and glorified, along with all who are in Christ Jesus. (See Romans chapter 8)

The truth of the matter is, if your pet has passed on then their spirit has already returned to the One who gave it — *God.* (See Ecclesiastes 12:7)

God's plan and desire is for you to ultimately go to where they are when your time is up and you leave this place. Knowing that they are safe and secure in heaven is wonderful, but the only way you will ever join them is if you make the decision to go there for yourself. Again, there is only one way that can happen, and that is by accepting Jesus Christ as your very own personal Savior.

In conclusion, the following verse of scripture settles the issue of reincarnation,

> *As it is appointed for men to die **once**,*
> *but after this comes the judgment,*
> (Hebrews 9:27 MEV)

THE REDEMPTIVE WORK OF CHRIST IS NOT LIMITED TO HUMANITY!

> For it pleased the Father that in Him all fullness should dwell,
> and to *RECONCILE* ALL THINGS to Himself by Him,
> having made peace through the blood of His cross, by Him,
> I say — whether they are *things* in earth, or *things* in heaven.
> (Colossians 1:19-20 MEV)

God's work of restoration through Jesus Christ was not just for humanity, but also for the entire created order. For God so loved the world (*Kosmos* — the entire created order) that He sent His only begotten Son... (John 3:16)

We know that animals have a special place, not only in man's past and present, but also in his future. Animals are God's idea. Genesis 1:28 assigned *man* the responsibility of taking care of them. But because of Adam's fall, the entire creation has suffered and looks forward to the sonship of redeemed man being revealed in its fullness. It's at that time when all of creation will be delivered "from the bondage of corruption into the glorious liberty of the children of God." (Romans 8:19-23) Animals will certainly be a part of the redeemed creation. (see Isaiah 65:25) They were created to glorify God and to be a permanent part of a creation that was intended to live forever.

Your pet's physical body will exist forever, just the same as your physical body will exist forever — because Jesus redeemed them with His Own blood on the cross at Calvary. After your pet has passed, there will come an appointed time when God will raise your pet's body up from the grave, and then take that very same body they once lived in and change it into a *glorified* condition. To be *glorified* means that their body will *magnify and bring glory and honor to God.*

Without a doubt our bodies are the most precious physical possession that we will ever have. They are a part of who we are and important to our identity. At the time of death or departure, the body doesn't want to let go because it was never designed to let go. Neither the body of a man or an animal is supposed to be separated from their spirit and soul. But no matter what you do, this physical body can only carry you so far. The day is going to come when this physical body cannot hold you here on this earth any longer, and that's the day that you breathe out your last breath. But death is not the end — it's not even the end of the physical body — it's just a *departure for a new beginning.* That's why you must make sure of where you will spend eternity.

Death is a door you go through by yourself. Jesus came to be the door to bring you into the glory of God. It is appointed unto men once to die, but after this the judgment. *You decide* — will you go up at the sound of that final trumpet?

> — *in a moment, in the twinkling of an eye, at the last trumpet.*
> *For the trumpet will sound,*
> *and the dead will be raised incorruptible, and we shall be changed.*
> (1 Corinthians 15:52 NKJV)

WHY WOULD GOD DELIVER THE ANIMALS OUT OF THE BONDAGE OF SIN AND NOT DELIVER THEM FROM DEATH?

HE WOULDN'T!

11

They are Not in Your Past

When a pet dies,
they're not in your past they're in your future —

But only,
if Jesus Christ is your Lord and Savior!

Nothing is more painful than the death of a loved one. When a pet is suddenly gone, their death leaves us feeling downcast, brokenhearted, grief-stricken, *and totally devastated.* The reason the pain of separation is so great, is because we were never meant to be separated — *death is unnatural.*

It is agonizing to have a pet die, but even more agonizing is the uncertainty of our pet's final destination. In actual fact, there are two things people want to know about their deceased loved ones — *where are they, and are they all right?*

The truth of the matter is, if your pet has died, *they are more than all right.* Think of it like this: if you were to leave your pet and go to a foreign county, who would you put in charge of their welfare? Where do you think they would be the safest — in a kennel, in the care of your family or friends, or in the presence of God who loves them more than you do?

For me, the answer would be God.

If you have ever experienced the death of a pet, then you know the grief that comes from the *sense of loss.* The spirit of grief *is the spirit of loss.* But regardless of what your feelings may be, the good news is, your pet is not lost at all — *and things couldn't be better for them.*

Animals are a part of the Kingdom of God and nothing is ever lost in the Kingdom of God

Once you discover the truth of where your pet has gone, you'll find comfort in knowing they're happy and whole in God's care. You'll stop referring to them as though they were lost somewhere, and in your past.

The language you use will no longer imply that your pet has ceased to exist, but rather it will affirm that they are very much alive. Your words will reflect the confident expectation that you have for a glorious future together.

When you realize that you *will* see your pet again, you'll stop thinking about them as though they no longer exist. You won't say things like, "My dog Beau, *used to be so smart...*," or "I really *loved* my cat Princess..."

Instead, you will refer to them in the present tense as though they were merely away, visiting another country. You'll say things like, "Beau *is* the smartest dog I've ever known and I'm excited about seeing him again," and "I *love* my Little Princess, but I miss her."

Whatever endearing attributes your pet had while they were with you — they still have!

It's important to get free from the lie that says your pet is stuck in your past somewhere, and you'll never have the opportunity to love them again.

Just because they've departed, doesn't mean your love for them stops. NO! The truth is, you still love them. *Love is eternal.*

A good example of this can be seen in the way we talk about our love for the Lord. We don't refer to Jesus in the past tense by saying, "I really *loved* Jesus." We talk about the Him as though He still exists, *because He does!* We speak in the present tense and say, "I *love* Jesus."

The same should be true when we talk about our pets and loved ones who have already departed. I still love my parents and I still love my pets. I expect to see them again after I depart. I know that our relationships will be even better than they were before. Remember, we are *all eternal beings* who one day will depart from this location and *simply move to another.*

The Apostle Paul refers to death as a departure, because — there is a destination after death
(See 2 Timothy 4:6)

So when you are born again and have an eternal perspective, you won't view your relationship with your pet as though they are *lost* somewhere in your past. Instead, you will be aware of the glorious future that you will have together.

However, this does not mean that you shouldn't enjoy the good memories that you have of your pets — *you absolutely should.* But at the same time, you need to be aware that Satan is a schemer. He will try to torment you with unpleasant thoughts and memories of past disappointments. He wants to put your mind and your heart in a dark place of desolation and absolute loss. He is a master of deception and he will twist the truth. His objective is to convince you that all is lost and there is no hope for a future with your pets — *he is a liar and the father of lies!*

Grief is the natural reaction to loss, whereas rejoicing is the supernatural response to the anticipation of a reunion

Therefore, refuse to look at what you think you've lost. Instead, look at what they've gained, as well as the time you've had with them. Get excited about the awesome future you will spend together. Do not focus on the idea that you did not get to say goodbye, but focus on the moment when you will get to say, HELLO!

You may miss them, but you haven't lost them. It's only a *temporary* separation. Remember, if you're born again and washed in the blood of the Lamb, then animals are not only in your past but also in your future.

When you get to the other side, you'll be in awe of the things that you will be able to do together —*nothing on earth can compare. There is no limit or end to the possibilities!*

So, if you enjoyed playing Frisbee with your dog, trail riding with your horse or just hanging out with your cat, and you feel as though you have been robbed of ever being able to do those things again — *you're wrong!*

Whatever the situation is that you believe you have missed out on… THAT'S THE POINT OF THIS CHAPTER — YOUR PETS ARE NOT LOST SOMEWHERE IN YOUR PAST!

If you choose to make the right decision with your own destiny — there is an awesome reunion waiting ahead for you!

Once you have a revelation of what I'm saying, you will never again refer to your pets as being lost. You will begin to get excited about what the future holds. You will think about all of the things you missed out on, but still want to do together. You will begin to realize that you have all of eternity to explore and experience new adventures that you never even dreamed were possible.

If your pet has already passed on, then your pet is more alive than ever

WHAT WILL THE FUTURE BE LIKE?

Beyond your wildest imagination! What you've experienced in the past is merely a shadow of what the future holds. You will interact on a level that is incomprehensible right now. Great things are in store. The center of your existence will be God because you will have been face to face with His love, which far exceeds anyone else's. God will be the center. Everything else revolves around Him. All other relationships, as awesome as they will be — will pale in comparison to God.

You will continue on with God's plan — restored and glorifying Him. All will glorify God. There will be no hindrances. There will be no fear — no worries — no competition — no pain — no sickness — no torment — no death. Total unity in God's Kingdom. No chaos — divine order and peace forever. Beauty — no wilted leaves or grass. No pollution — no anger — only love in God's Kingdom. Splendor — activities — joy — worship — relationships — laughter. You will do things that were never possible before.

God's animals are forever free from abuse in heaven and on the New Earth. It will be what God planned from the beginning. Sin has perverted God's plan but restoration is coming. This life is but a vapor.

We will recognize and know one another on a greater level than is possible now. Much was lost in the fall that we have never seen or experienced together. All will be restored. You will play together and love one another. Love never ends. Freedom unlike ever experienced before. Expectation! Look forward. Expect. Set your heart on what's to come. Don't believe the lie of the devil that it's over — NO, not at all. It's a new beginning! Don't believe that they're lost — God doesn't lose what's His!

So the point of this chapter is…YES! Your pets can be in your future — that is, if you choose to go where they go. We are all eternal beings and we will all reside somewhere when we leave our bodies. The truth is, you were never meant to be separated from your loved ones — even your furry, feathered ones — just as, *you were never meant to be separated from God.*

The only way you won't see animals in heaven is — if you don't get there yourself

When you feel powerless to change the situation, it leaves you with a sense of hopelessness — but it doesn't have to be that way. By *situation*, I mean the *belief* that you are permanently separated from your pets.

The truth is, *you are not powerless.* You have the power to change the situation, simply by making a decision. The decision is the one where you choose Jesus Christ to be your personal Lord and Savior. And when you do, *hope replaces hopelessness.*

Without Jesus Christ and the finished work of the cross — there is NO HOPE of a future reconciliation with your pets or anyone else. And even worse than that, without Jesus Christ and the finished work of the cross — there is NO HOPE of reconciliation with a loving God!

It's a time to choose. For those who reject Jesus Christ, they will never see animals again. They are God's animals and they are returning to Him. Eternal separation from God also means eternal separation from His animals. There is no other way, except through Jesus Christ. Man can't set the rules — only God. And God is a loving and just God.

MAN'S WAYS LEAD TO A HOPELESS END —
GOD'S WAY LEADS TO ENDLESS HOPE!
~Author Unknown

12

The Joy of the Reunion

Joy unspeakable and full of glory…

(1 PETER 1:8 KJV)

Many times people have tried to console me about the death of a pet by sending me a copy of a poem called, "The Rainbow Bridge." Even though there is a comforting message in the poem, the message is misleading. Let me explain what I mean after we take a look at what the poem actually says.

The Original Rainbow Bridge Poem

Just this side of heaven is a place called Rainbow Bridge.
When an animal dies that has been especially close to someone
here, that pet goes to Rainbow Bridge. There are meadows
and hills for all of our special friends so they can run and play
together. There is plenty of food, water and sunshine, and our
friends are warm and comfortable.

All the animals who had been ill and old are restored to health
and vigor. Those who were hurt or maimed are made whole and
strong again, just as we remember them in our dreams of days
and times gone by.

The animals are happy and content, except for one small thing;
they each miss someone very special to them, who had to be left behind.

They all run and play together, but the day comes when one
suddenly stops and looks into the distance. His bright eyes are
intent. His eager body quivers. Suddenly he begins to run from
the group, flying over the green grass, his legs carrying him
faster and faster.

You have been spotted, and when you and your special friend
finally meet, you cling together in joyous reunion, never to be
parted again. The happy kisses rain upon your face; your hands
again caress the beloved head, and you look once more into the
trusting eyes of your pet, so long gone from your life never
absent from your heart.

Then you cross Rainbow Bridge together, never again to be separated.
~ Author unknown

Although the above scenario may sound wonderful, it is not a true
picture of what the reunion between you and your pets will look like.

To begin with, there is no such thing in the Bible as *Rainbow Bridge*. However, there are several references to the rainbow.

The rainbow represents a promise from God that He will never again destroy the earth by a flood

The first mention of a rainbow begins in Genesis 9:8, which tells us that the rainbow is a *sign of the covenant* that God made with both man and animals. But nowhere in the Bible does it say that the rainbow is a bridge. The Scripture below is what the Bible says concerning the rainbow and the covenant that God made with both man and the animals.

> Then God spoke to Noah and to his sons with him, saying: "And as for Me, behold, I establish My covenant with you and with your descendants after you, *and with every living creature* that is with you: the birds, the cattle, and every beast of the earth with you, of all that go out of the ark, every beast of the earth. Thus I establish My covenant with you: Never again shall all flesh be cut off by the waters of the flood; never again shall there be a flood to destroy the earth."
>
> And God said: "*This is the sign of the covenant* which I make between Me and you, *and every living creature that is with you,* for perpetual generations: I set My *rainbow* in the cloud, and it shall be for the sign of the covenant between Me and the earth. It shall be, when I bring a cloud over the earth, that the *rainbow* shall be seen in the cloud; and I will remember My covenant which is between Me and you *and every living creature of all flesh*; the waters shall never again become a flood to destroy all flesh. The *rainbow* shall be in the cloud, and I will look on it to remember *the everlasting covenant between God and every living creature of all flesh that is on the earth.*" And God said to Noah, "*This is the sign of the covenant which I have established between Me and all flesh that is on the earth.*" (Genesis 9:8-17 NKJV)

The rainbow is the sign of God's covenant — Not an actual bridge that you and your pet will cross over

Now, what is true about this poem is the part that says, "All the animals who had been ill and old are restored to health and vigor. Those who were hurt or maimed are made whole and strong again, just as we remember them in our dreams of days and times gone by."

But, the problem with this poem is; it leaves out the one essential requirement necessary for those who really do want to go to heaven and reunite with their pets. Nowhere in this poem does it tell the reader that in order to go to Heaven and forever be with their pets in the afterlife, that they must be saved or *born again*. Instead, the reader is led to believe that *no matter what,* they will meet their pets again at Rainbow Bridge and they will never be separated. This simply is not true.

Not everyone is going to heaven, and those who don't will never see their pets again!

The part that was left out of the Rainbow Bridge poem is the most important part — *Jesus Christ. Without Him, there is no hope of being reunited with your pets —ever!*

Unless you choose to accept Jesus Christ as your personal Savior — There will be no reunion in heaven with God or your pets!

Now as awesome as heaven is, we should not focus on *the place,* but rather on reconciling back to God. *Reuniting with God will be the most significant and exciting thing about going to heaven!*

Heaven is a real place, and it's for the redeemed!

WHAT WILL THE REUNION BE LIKE?

Under the inspiration of the Holy Spirit, the following description was given to me about what I can expect the reunion between my beloved animals, my family, my friends and myself to be like:

*"Ecstasy — **total bliss** —is what you will experience. In My glory — in the midst, you will know what you've never dreamed — you will know. You will share in an intimacy like never before — pure and*

*holy — mutual admiration — contentment like you've never known.
You will know each other on a level that will be supernatural. There
will be a knowing — like you know, that you know, that you know.
You'll know what you've never known before. Your bond and connection will be one with the assurance that it will never ever be broken
— eternal.*

*You cannot understand this now with only your natural mind but the
Spirit in you knows, and He will show and tell you what you ask. You
will talk about many things — you will do things together that you never did before. Your hearts will know that you will never again be torn
apart. Your lives will continue on to greater heights. Your communication will be unhindered by sin. Your expression of one another will be
enhanced. Life will be perfect — and you will be perfected. Your reunion
and your relationship will glorify Me. I will be at the center. I AM the
source for all true happiness and joy. You will know and understand one
another unlike anything you ever imagined. Communication will be
restored. Love will be perfected — pure and holy.*

*Divine relationships will never be broken. It will be unlike any
reunion anyone has ever known on earth. The Kiss of heaven will
be upon it! Sealed by mutual Agape love. No questions — no doubts
— no uncertainties —blessed assurance. Unwavering! Purpose will
become crystal clear — there will be no unhappy memories —only
joyous expectations. Have delight for it's true for those who love Me.
Those who will stand for Me. The appointed time will be nothing
short of miraculous.*

*The crowds will be gathered to welcome and usher you in. My ani-
mals are among Me. They worship Me — They love Me — They are
in My presence — it may surprise some to know this but they are an
important part of My Kingdom.*

*You care for them well — I Am grateful that you take responsibil-
ity and care and pray over them. They are grateful too —Yes, they
know — more than you know they know. Your heart knows the truth
well — don't figure this out with your head — listen with your heart*

— I Am an eternal God and I did not make disposable animals or people. Your purpose with the animals is eternal — your gifts are eternal. Your heart knows that well — you will be forever with those I have entrusted into your care.

Your relationship with them on the other side will be magnified and intensified by My glory. They will always be special to you and you will always be special to them. Everything that was caused by sin will be gone — it will be restored better than it ever was in the beginning. I Am God — and I perfect My creation that loves Me. Great and mighty things are in "store"— Only believe!"

13

God Created Animals
for a Reason

CONCLUSION

It was not for exploitation
And it was not for them to be worshiped!

I was working with the horses one day when out of nowhere, the Lord asked me this question, *"Caren, why did I create animals?"*

At first I wondered: *Why would He ask me that? He knows I know the answer — it's a "no-brainer."* But then I thought, *Uh-oh, God doesn't ask insignificant, meaningless questions. I must be missing something.*

As I pondered over His question for a few minutes, I thought to myself,

Oh my, I'm not sure I want to answer this. I don't know exactly what it is, but there's just something about the way He asked, that leads me to believe that I might not know. Anything that has to do with the animals is important to me — what if I've been wrong?

Then right in the midst of my internal conversation, I was suddenly aware of the fact that God was listening to my every thought. I remember saying to myself, *I wish I could hide what I'm thinking.*

Now I know that God is never critical, but even so I was still somewhat disappointed and even a bit embarrassed by my lack of knowledge concerning a subject so dear to me.

When I finally did answer I said, "Okay Lord, I think you created them to be man's companions."

God immediately replied, *"That's not why I created animals. That's a benefit, that's a* **by-product** *— but that is not why I created them."*

It got quiet, and while I was somewhat frozen in place, God asked me again, *"Why did I create the animals?"*

Without hesitation, I admitted that I really didn't know why, and asked Him to please tell me.

His answer was simple and yet profound, **"*I created the animals to glorify Me!*"**

Since then, I've asked a number of people that same question. The majority of responses were similar to the following statements: "For our enjoyment," "for our companionship," "to show us His love," and "for our protection."

Not one person gave as their answer, "To glorify God." Not one! Every response was *self-centered.*

Insofar as it pertains to the animals, it seems to me that our world revolves around *self.* Even though the above statements about the animals are true, they are merely *benefits* and *byproducts,* and not the central focus. God's purpose for creating animals is far greater than any one of us can truly fathom.

Like others, I had no idea that I was self-centered concerning the purpose for the creation of animals; it had never occurred to me. At least, not until the Lord pointed it out to me with the following loving rebuke;

"That's not why I created animals. That's a *benefit,* that's a *byproduct* — but that is not why I created them. *It's not all about you Caren. It's really not all about you.* I created the animals to glorify Me. And that's why I created man — to glorify Me!"

SO, WHAT DOES IT MEAN TO GLORIFY GOD?

It means to praise, to magnify and honor Him in worship. It means to exalt, extol, reverence, adore, and give thanks to Him for Who He is and what He has done. And it means to be obedient to both His written and His spoken word. *To me, it means to know Him and love Him above everything. Glorifying God is a heart attitude!*

We glorify God when we let His presence be known

John the Apostle, gave us a perfect example of animals glorifying God in the Book of *Revelation.* Through a vision, he saw four animals worshiping both day and night around the throne of God — giving Him glory, honor and thanks as they declared:

> "Holy, holy, holy,
> Lord God Almighty,
> Who was and is and is to come!"
> (Revelation 4:8 NKJV)

Not only did John witness the animals around the throne, but he also saw twenty-four elders worshiping and proclaiming:

> "You are worthy, O Lord, To receive glory and honor and power;
> For You created all things,
> And by Your will they exist and were created."
> (Revelation 4:11 NKJV)

Psalm 148 commands all of creation to praise the Lord, *including the animals:*

> Animals and all cattle, creeping things and flying birds;
> kings of the earth and all peoples, princes and all rulers of the earth;
> both young men and maidens, old men and children.

> Let them praise the name of the Lord, for His name alone is excellent;
> His glory is above the earth and heaven.
> (Psalm 148:10-13 MEV)

We find animals worshipping God throughout the Bible, both in heaven and on the earth.

Psalm 150 is *another* example that points to the fact that animals were created to glorify God:

> Let *everything* that has breath praise the Lord. Praise the Lord!
> (Psalm 150:6 NKJV)

Animals have breath! *Everything includes animals. Therefore...*

...Animals were created to glorify God!

As I mentioned earlier, we also glorify God through obedience. Jesus said to His Father, *"I have glorified You on the earth. I have finished the work which You have given Me to do."* (John 17:4 NKJV)

It may come as a surprise to some, but animals also obey God.

- It was God who told the fish to vomit out Jonah onto dry land.
- It was God who commanded the ravens to feed the prophet, Elijah.
- And it was God who instructed the animals to go into the Ark.

Again, obedience glorifies God, and animals glorify God through obedience!

It's interesting that when Jesus obeyed God, *man benefited*. When the animals obeyed God, *man benefited*. And when we obey God, *man benefits*.

The truth is, everything was created for God's glory and exists to glorify Him. Nothing exists for itself. Now this does not mean God's glory is *narcissistic* or that He is some sort of an egotistical glory *monger*. He alone is "*El Shaddai*," God Almighty — The All-Sufficient One!

God doesn't require anything from anyone to be Who He is.

We glorify God *because of Who He is — not to make Him Who He is.*

The message of this book is simple. God loves His creation! **All life is valuable and precious to Him — both human life and animal life.**

God was glorified at the consummation of creation, and the result was that *all of creation benefited*. Then sin altered the perfect picture. The fall of man caused a curse to come upon the entire creation, resulting in sickness, disease and death — *bringing no glory to God.* Creation was doomed and unable to help itself.

But wait, God has a plan! It's a plan of salvation that brings redemption and restoration to the *entire creation*. You're an important part of His plan — the animals are an important part of His plan — and the earth is an important part of His plan.

If God's plan had failed to include the animals that would mean the innocent are not worthy to be redeemed, but the guilty are. It would mean that there is no justice where the animals are concerned. It would mean that they are unimportant to God. And it would mean that part of God's original plan failed.

If the animals were annihilated or simply ceased to exist, that would mean man's sin triumphed over the animals. It would also mean that the fall of man has the power to prevent the animals from glorifying God throughout all of eternity. But thank God that is not what's true. The fact of the matter is, *God is glorified in the redemption of the animals —* and God will be glorified in the resurrection of their bodies — and God will be glorified in the reunion between mankind and their beloved pets. *God's Perfect Eternal Plan* would be incomplete without the animals.

The eternal destiny of an animal is untouchable by man's sin!

The Lord said to me one day, *"I didn't lose anything to Satan. That would have made Satan the victor. I don't lose what is Mine."*

I responded with the following question, *"But Lord, how can I ever say that? When we talk about all of the lost in hell, doesn't that mean Satan won?"* He replied, *"Satan did not have the victory over them — they chose! There's a difference. I didn't lose them!* **I made a way for them and they chose to walk away.**"

As far as the animals are concerned, Satan didn't win there either. The Bible says they belong to God and God doesn't lose what is His.

Now it's true that the animals have been made to suffer the consequences of man's sin, but *they themselves are not held responsible for the debt of man's sin.* This one significant fact places them in an entirely different category from mankind. And the difference is, *man is accountable for his sin and must have a Savior to rescue his soul from eternal damnation.*

Remember, God doesn't lose what belongs to Him! If you want to become a born again child of God, you do that by receiving Jesus Christ as your personal Lord and Savior — *that's all there is to it!*

It's your choice! You will never be able to stand before a holy God, a righteous judge — **and you will stand** — but you'll not stand there and be able to say that you did not have a fair shake at this. *You cannot even blame Satan if you choose to reject Jesus Christ.* **God gave you your own free will!**

What Jesus did on the cross went beyond saving the soul of man to the *redeeming of an entire kingdom that was lost*. That kingdom includes man, animals and all of creation.

Jesus redeemed on the cross everything that Adam lost in the fall.

Had Jesus not done what He did at the cross, every man's soul would be eternally condemned.

Had He not done what He did at the cross, animals would not get their physical bodies back.

Had He not done what He did at the cross, animals would not be able to be put back into right relationship with man.

Had He not done what He did at the cross, the spirit and soul of an animal would return to God without ever reuniting with man. This would mean that the animals would not have a future of fellowship with man on the earth — *forfeiting God's original design.*

And, had Jesus not done what He did at the cross, only man along with the fallen angels would have ended up in eternal damnation.

Heaven has animals — Hell does not!

You will never have an eternal relationship with your pets outside of a personal relationship with Jesus Christ! So, who is Jesus Christ to you? Is He merely a good man, a Samaritan, a prophet, a teacher? Or is He the Son of God and your personal Lord and Savior? The Bible says He's all those things — but is He your Lord, is He your Savior? The animals know Him as Lord. But who is Jesus Christ to YOU?

Heaven is real and Hell is real — you alone decide your eternal destination.

When you receive Jesus Christ as your personal Lord and Savior, *God is glorified!*

The benefit is not only eternal security, but also Eternity with Your Pets.

You alone have the power to secure your eternal destiny by praying a simple prayer from your heart.

And that every tongue should confess that Jesus Christ is Lord, to the glory of God the Father.
(Philippians 2:11 KJV)

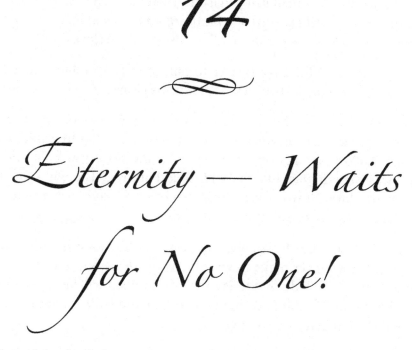

14

Eternity — Waits for No One!

We have it backwards in debating whether or not animals are going to be in heaven. The real question is — *will you be there?*

The most important decision a person could ever make, is the one where they decide where they will spend eternity.

Maybe you've read this book, but you've never surrendered your life to Jesus. Let me ask you life's most crucial question: *If you were to die in the middle of the night — where would you go?* Do you know without a shadow of doubt, where you would spend eternity? Is your name written in the Lambs Book of Life? The question is — *Are you born again?*

If you're reading this now, you still have a chance to choose between eternal life and eternal damnation —*the power is in your hands.* As long as you have the breath of life in you, you have the opportunity to choose your destiny. Don't miss the moment, *tomorrow might be too late!* Today the Lord gives you the opportunity to surrender your life to Him. Today is the day of salvation. Jesus calls you. Just say, *Lord here I am. I give you my life — take it!* He'll take what's broken, battered, twisted and torn and He'll make something beautiful out of it, if you'll only surrender to Him. If you'll come to Him and say, *Lord I'm tired of a life of self and sin, and today I surrender my life to You. Please forgive me.* He'll do just that. Jesus loves you!

I want you to know, there is a Heaven to gain and a Hell to shun. There is no purgatory. There is no in-between. The choice is Heaven or the choice is Hell.

It doesn't matter who you are or what you've done — God loves you and He has a great plan for your life. You don't have to go to a devil's hell because 2,000 years ago on Calvary's cross the price was paid and the blood was shed. It's just like that old song that says, "There is a fountain filled with blood drawn from Emmanuel's veins, and sinners plunged beneath that flood lose all their guilty stains."

Jesus said to come as little children with a childlike faith. The greatest decision you will ever make in your life is the decision to turn your life over to God. If you'll do that today, the power of sin will be broken off of you. The power of guilt and shame will be removed from your life and you will be changed — *never to be the same.*

The Lord loves you and stands with arms wide open and says, "Come to Me, all you who labor and are heavy laden, and I will give you rest." He says, "Take My yoke upon you and learn from Me... For My yoke is easy and My burden is light."

For God so loved the world that He gave His only begotten Son that whosoever shall believe in Him shall not perish but have everlasting life. For God did *not* send His Son into the world to *condemn* the world but that the world through Him might be *saved.*

You can't buy salvation — you can't earn salvation. You just have to humble yourself and receive it. The Bible says, "for all have sinned and come short of the glory of God." It tells us, "for the wages of sin is death but the gift of God is eternal life through Jesus Christ our Lord." And it promises us — that *whosoever* calls upon the name of the Lord shall be saved. *You are a whosoever!*

Jesus is calling you now. He said He will take out the stony heart and put in a heart of flesh. He said a new spirit will I put within you. He loves you so very much. Will you surrender your life to Him today?

I'm not talking about religion. It's easy to be religious, but being religious is not being spiritual. I'm talking about a relationship with God. You can know that you know, you are a child of God.

I want to invite you to pray the greatest prayer in the world. It's called the sinner's prayer. Saying words alone will not save you. But if you have faith in what they mean, then the blood of Jesus Christ, God's Son will wash away every sin. *If you want to be born again and have the assurance of eternal life with your pets in heaven,* then repeat the following prayer out loud and believe in your heart what God said in His word is true.

Dear God in heaven, I come to you in the name of Your Son Jesus. I'm sorry for my sin — the things that I have done, please forgive me and cleanse me with your precious blood from all unrighteousness. Lord you said in Your word, if I confess with my mouth, Jesus is my Lord and my Savior, and I believe in my heart that God has raised You from the dead — I will be saved. So Father right now, I confess, that Jesus Christ has come in the flesh. He is my Lord and my Savior. Come into my heart right now, take out the stony heart, put in a heart of flesh. Forgive me of my sin. Wash me, cleanse me, change me, fill me, use me. Let me never be the same again. Fill me with the Holy Spirit and the joy of the Lord. I turn my back on the world. I turn my back on sin. And I follow You Lord Jesus.

Thank You for dying for me. Thank You for shedding Your blood for me. Thank You that on the third day You rose for me. And thank You that you're coming back again for me. By faith, in the finished work of the cross and by the shed blood of Jesus, I receive now, the free gift of salvation. I'm forgiven. I'm born again. I'm a new creation in Christ Jesus. I am saved! Thank You Lord, for saving me now.

If you prayed that prayer from your heart that means you've accepted Jesus Christ as your Lord and Savior. I want to encourage you to get a Bible and begin to read the Book of John, the Book of Acts and then find a local church that believes the full gospel — *that Jesus saves, heals, sets free, delivers, baptizes in the Holy Ghost and that He's coming very, very soon.*

TO GOD BE THE GLORY!

15

What the Bible Says about Animals

For every wild animal of the forest is Mine,
and the cattle on a thousand hills.

I know every bird of the mountains,
and the creatures that move in the field are Mine.

(PSALM 50:10-11 MEV)

Whether wild or tame — *all animals belong to God.* Our relationship
with them is one of stewardship, not ownership.

God cares about the animals and provides for their every need

The eyes of all look expectantly to You,
And You give them their food in due season.
You open Your hand
And satisfy the desire of every living thing.
(Psalm 145:15-16 NKJV)

It is God who sustains all life

We tend to think that the animals adapted to their habitat, but it was actually the other way around. The earth was made to accommodate the needs of the animals. The psalmist declares that *creation was not only made for man but also for the animals*

You send the springs to gush forth in the valleys,
which flow between the hills.
They give drink to every animal of the field:
the wild donkeys quench their thirst.
By them the birds of the heavens have their habitation;
they sing among the branches.
You water the mountains from Your lofty chamber;
the earth is satisfied with the fruit of Your works.
You cause the grass to grow for the cattle
and plants for the cultivation of man,
that he may bring forth food from the earth
and wine that makes glad the heart of man,
and oil that makes shine his face,
and bread that strengthens his heart.
The trees of the Lord are well watered,
the cedars of Lebanon that He has planted,
where the birds make their nests,
where the stork has its home in the fir trees.
The high mountains are for the wild goats,
and the rocks a refuge for the badgers.
(Psalm 104:10-18 MEV)

Both man and animals can rely on the providence of God

Then He said to His disciples,

> "Therefore I say to you, do not worry about your life, what you will eat;
> nor about the body, what you will put on. Life is more than food,
> and the body is more than clothing.
> *Consider the ravens, for they neither sow nor reap,*
> *which have neither storehouse nor barn; and God feeds them.*
> Of how much more value are you than the birds?" (Luke 12:22-24 NKJV)

There was no killing of animals for food before the fall of man

In the beginning, one of the first things God did was provide food for *all of creation.*

> The God said, "See, I have given you every plant yielding seed
> which is on the face of all the earth and every tree
> which has fruit yielding seed. It shall be food for you.
> To every beast of the earth and to every bird of the air
> and to everything that creeps on the earth which
> has the **breath of life** in it, I have given every green
> plant for food." And it was so.
> (Genesis 1:29-30 MEV)

God saves animals and humans alike

> Your righteousness is like the great mountains,
> Your judgments like the great deep;
> O Lord, You *preserve man and beast.*
> (Psalm 36:6 MEV)

That word "preserve" means to *rescue, save and bring victory.* The word "beast" refers to *animals.*

Notice: It does **not** say, O Lord, You *destroy or annihilate* both man and beast!

Below is another passage of Scripture that confirms — God preserves *all of creation.*

You alone are the Lord. You have made heaven,
the heaven of heavens, with all their host,
the earth and *all that is on it,* the seas and *all that is in them;*
and *You preserve them all.* And the host of heaven worships You.
(Nehemiah 9:6 MEV)

Animals are valuable to God and a part of His eternal plan.

God expects man to help ALL animals if they are in trouble

When it comes to the welfare of an animal, God told us to always do what is in the best interest of the animal, even if the animal belongs to an enemy. We are expected to lay aside any personal vendettas and put the needs of the animal first. That is, help the person whose animal is in trouble, even if the person is someone who hates us. *Regardless of the situation, take care of God's animals!*

If you meet your enemy's ox or his donkey going astray,
you shall surely bring it back to him again.

If you see the donkey of one who hates you
lying [helpless] under his load, you shall refrain
from leaving the man to cope with it alone;
you shall help him to release the animal.
(Exodus 23:4-5 AMPC)

Solomon said in the Book of Proverbs, that the nature of a man is revealed by the way he treats an animal

A righteous man regards the life of his animal,
But the tender mercies of the wicked are cruel.
(Proverbs 12:10 NKJV)

We will all give an account one day for the way we have treated the animals. Plain and simple, it is a sin to abuse or mistreat any animal!

God abhors animal abuse and cruelty

We are told in the Book of Deuteronomy that man is to never muzzle an ox while it works. This justifiably shows compassion for the ox by permitting him to be free to eat while he works. (See Deuteronomy 25:4)

God's word is clear; man should never take advantage of his superior position over animals.

Animals played a part in God's decision to spare the city of Nineveh

"Should I not, therefore, be concerned about Nineveh,
that great city, in which there are more than a hundred and
twenty thousand people, who do not know their right hand
from their left, *and also many animals?*"
(Jonah 4:11 MEV)

It should not surprise us that God is concerned about the lives of the animals, after all, they do belong to Him. Remember what He said; "For every wild animal of the forest is Mine, and the cattle on a thousand hills. I know every bird of the mountains, and the creatures that move in the field are Mine. (Psalm 50:10-11 MEV)

God sees the life of every created being

And there is no *creature* hidden from His sight,
but all things are naked and open to the eyes of Him
to whom *we must give account.* (Hebrews 4:13 NKJV)

It is God's will that every animal have a name

In Biblical days, names had meaning and carried identity. In the Old Testament the word *name* means to convey honor, character and authority.

From the very beginning, it was God who established the use of names. He gave Adam the responsibility of naming not just a few of the animals, *but each and every one of them.*

Names have meaning! When Adam declared their name, he was actually assigning to them the very character and authority of that name.

> So Adam gave names to *all* cattle,
> to the birds of the air,
> and to *every* beast of the field…
> (Genesis 2:20 NKJV)

In the above verse we find that Adam not only gave group names to birds such as sparrows and eagles, but that he named each and every one of them — *individually*. Likewise, he did the same with horses, cows, fish and all of God's creatures. It was not just a *classification* when he named them, *it was personal*. There is no doubt that Adam had a personal and unique relationship with each and every animal. That has been God's intention from the beginning; nothing has changed and nothing will change throughout eternity.

> Out of the ground the Lord God formed every beast
> of the field and every bird of the air,
> and brought them to Adam to see what he would call them.
> And whatever Adam called *each living creature,*
> that was its name. (Genesis 2:19 NKJV)

The job of naming the animals was not just some frivolous exercise, but a very important part of the plan of God. Even today, the names that we give to animals are a precious gift because they are essential and personal.

Names will always be important because they not only carry meaning, but animals also identify with their individual name. And not only do they respond to their name, but they also recognize the names of people and other animals with whom they have a relationship. Suffice it to say, animals would never be able to comprehend these various names unless they had a soul — *giving them the ability to reason.*

Adam was given the privilege of naming the animals because they are a central and significant part of creation. We do the same thing today, and when we do we are establishing a relationship and connecting with them on a personal level.

 Eternity with Your Pets

Each and every name has meaning, and the very character and nature of the animal is reflected in their name. So, when you give your pet a name, you should know the meaning of that name, *and seriously consider the impact that name will have on your pet.*

Animals are great teachers

The book of Job tells us that animals have an amazing ability to effectively communicate as well as teach. The following verses show us the profound insight that Job had into the animal kingdom.

> "But now ask the beasts, and they will teach you;
> And the birds of the air, and they will tell you;
> Or speak to the earth, and it will teach you;
> And the fish of the sea will explain to you.
> Who among all these does not know
> That the hand of the Lord has done this,
> *In whose hand is the life of every living thing,*
> And the breath of all mankind?"
> (Job 12:7-10 NKJV)

The above portion of Scripture reveals that animals know that their lives are in the hands of God, whereas man does not always have this understanding.

Animals will teach us, if we will only pay attention!

Ants teach us life skills

Proverbs is a book in the Bible known for insightful wisdom, and one of the proverbs instructs us to pay attention to the ant. If we do, we will learn some valuable lessons that will help us in our own lives.

Ants are clever little hard workers who successfully manage themselves and they answer to no one. King Solomon, one of the wisest men who ever lived, said the following about the ant,

> Go to the ant, you sluggard!
> Consider her ways and be wise,

Which, having no captain,
Overseer or ruler,
Provides her supplies in the summer,
And gathers her food in the harvest.
(Proverbs 6:6-8 NKJV)

That's quite an impressive work ethic! We can see that ants are not only smart but also hard workers who know how to implement their plans. They are so wise and diligent in their accomplishments that the lazy, slothful man is advised to study them and learn from their way of life.

Have you ever learned from an animal?

I clearly remember my own experience as a child when I took my dog to obedience school. I was super excited about all of the things *he* was going to learn.

After the trainer introduced herself, she began the class by explaining who the students were. To my surprise, it was not our dogs — *but us!*

Me and mom getting Smokey ready.

That seemed foolish to me so I immediately began to doubt her teaching ability. I thought to myself, *what am I doing here?* It seemed to me that the instructor was the one who needed to go to school.

My dog Smokey, was a Siberian Husky with a sweet disposition. However, he had a mind of his own and an independent nature that often got us both into deep trouble. That's why I signed *him* up for the class. *He was the one who needed to learn how to listen and behave, not me!*

Now I didn't want to embarrass myself by abruptly leaving the class, so I decided to stick it out and stay that day. As it turns out, I'm glad that I did.

To my surprise, I discovered that what I thought was disobedience on my dogs part, was actually a lack of communication on my part. I had disciplined Smokey from my perspective without understanding what was behind his behavior. I had missed what he was saying to me and it was through the help of the dog trainer that I began to understand his language.

The more I understood, the more obvious it became to me that Smokey *never did anything out of spite.* Unlike people, animals don't have ulterior motives. (See the chapter, "No Guilt, No Pride, No Shame.")

By listening to my dog, I discovered that what the Bible says is true —

— Animals do in fact, make great teachers

Animals teach us to trust God

In the New Testament, Jesus explained to His disciples that they could trust their heavenly Father for all of their needs. Oddly enough, it was the birds that He used as an example. He told the disciples that the birds neither sow nor reap, nor gather food to store for their future yet they know how to trust God, who always provides for them.

The point that Jesus emphasized was that the birds were already doing what the disciples needed to do. Namely — *trust God with their lives.* (See Matthew 6:26-30 NKJV)

When we feed the birds, we're actually doing the work of the Lord.

Animals submit to authority, but man rebels against God!

> The ox knows his owner,
> and the donkey his master's crib,
> but Israel does not know;
> My people do not consider.
> (Isaiah 1:3 MEV)

Birds know and understand their divine destiny

"Even the stork in the heavens knows her appointed times; and the turtledove, the swift, and the swallow observe the time of their coming. But My people do not know the judgment of the Lord. (Jeremiah 8:7 NKJV)

Animals listen to, and obey God

In 1 Kings 17:4, the Lord declares, " *...I have commanded the ravens to feed you there."*

The ravens brought food *every* day to the prophet Elijah. It was not by chance or coincidence but by the command of God. The ravens heard what God told them and fed the hungry prophet, *twice a day.*

Animals heard God's call of salvation, but man ignored His invitation

God had Noah build an ark to save the people and the animals. While preparing the ark Noah preached, but no one accepted God's plan of salvation. However, the animals heard and obeyed God and were saved with Noah's family.

> And they went into the ark to Noah, two by two, of
> all flesh in which is the breath of life...as God had
> commanded him; (Genesis 7:15-16 NKJV)

It was a dove who looked after man's welfare

Noah released a dove from the ark who not only had the intelligence but also the compassion to bring back an olive branch, communicating to Noah that it would soon be safe to unload. (See Genesis 8:11 NKJV)

Horses are eternal spirit beings

In the Book of Revelation, John describes the imminent return of The Lord Jesus Christ as it was revealed to him in a vision.

> I saw heaven opened. And there was a white horse.
> He who sat on it is called Faithful and True,
> and in righteousness He judges and wages war…
> The armies in heaven, clothed in fine linen,
> white and clean, followed Him on white horses.
> (Revelation 19:11,14 MEV)

Horses are a part of God's heavenly army

The Lord Jesus will soon return to earth and set up His kingdom where He will rule and reign as King of Kings and Lord of Lords. And when He does return it will be on none other than a white horse. This in itself speaks volumes regarding the high esteem and importance that Jesus places on horses!

If the horses in heaven are spirit beings, then why wouldn't the horses and other animals who are on the earth also be spirit beings?

BE AWARE: Before the imminent return of the Lord Jesus Christ, there is coming another rider on a white horse. The Bible says in Revelation 6:2,

> And I looked, and there before me was a white horse.
> He who sat on it had a bow.
> And a crown was given to him,
> and he went forth conquering that he might overcome. (MEV)

DO NOT BE DUPED — the rider on this white horse is a counterfeit of the Christ, and is referred to as the Anti-Christ — man of sin. *This man will be the final world dictator —one seeking global dominion.*

Observe that this rider has a bow, but *no arrows.*

As the world increasingly looks for some form of *global peace,* the Bible warns us that this man is an *imposter* and he will deceive and fool many by impersonating the true *Prince of Peace — Jesus Christ.*

Horses are mentioned extensively in the Bible — over 150 times!

Another example that proves the existence of horses in the spirit realm is found in 2 Kings 2:11. In this historical account we are told how two prophets, Elijah and Elisha were supernaturally separated by a chariot of fire and horses of fire. The Bible describes it this way;

> Then it happened, as they continued on and talked,
> that suddenly a chariot of fire appeared with horses of fire,
> and separated the two of them;
> and Elijah went up by a whirlwind into heaven. (2 Kings 2:11 NKJV)

Unseen power of God

Later on in the life of Elisha, we find a second occurrence that also involved supernatural horses. This event took place when the king of Syria waged war against Israel.

Elisha was in Dothan, an ancient city of Israel, when Syria's king sent out his army with horses and chariots to capture him. They surrounded the city at night, and by early morning Elisha and his servant awoke in the middle of a great siege.

Terrified by the situation, the servant thought that they were hopelessly outnumbered. But the man of God, Elisha, knew differently.

Having an understanding that could only have come from God, the prophet comforted his servant with the following words, "Do not fear, *for those who are with us are more than those who are with them.*" (2 Kings 6:16 NKJV)

And then moved by compassion for his servant, Elisha prayed and asked God to open the servant's eyes to allow him to see the truth of what was taking place in the spirit realm.

God answered the prophet's prayer and gave the man the supernatural ability to see what had existed in the spirit realm all along. And the servant saw...

"...the mountain was full of *horses* and chariots of fire all around Elisha."
(2 Kings 6:17 NKJV)

**If heaven has horses
why wouldn't other animals be there as well?**

IMPORTANT FACT: When we see the word "beast" or "living creatures" in the Book of Revelation, we can substitute the word "animal."

The reason these words were used is because the King James translation had no term for ANIMAL.

However, there is one exception to this statement and that exception is when the word "beast" is referring to the "anti-christ." (See Revelation 13:1-4 NKJV)

So, as you read the following portions of Scripture, substitute the word "animal" where ever it says, "living creatures" and you will get a better understanding of what's being said.

Animals are in the midst of the throne of God

> Before the throne there was a sea of glass, like crystal.
> And in the midst of the throne, and around the throne,
> were four *living creatures* full of eyes in front and in back.
> The first *living creature* was *like a lion*, the second living
> creature *like a calf,* the third living creature had a face
> *like a man,* and the fourth living creature was
> *like a flying eagle.* (Revelation 4:6-7 NKJV)

The "four living creatures" in the above reference all have different faces. Each face represents a different aspect of creation. The lion represents the wild animals. The calf represents domestic animals. The eagle is symbolic of the birds and the man represents mankind. Collectively, they represent the whole of creation.

Think about it — there are animals leading worship around the throne of God!

I don't think people realize that the *living creatures* who are giving God glory, honor and thanks in heaven, *are animals.*

> *Holy, holy, holy, is the Lord God Almighty,*
> *who was and is and is to come!*

> Whenever the **living creatures** give glory and honor
> and thanks to Him who sits on the throne, who lives
> forever and ever, the twenty-four elders fall down before
> Him who sits on the throne and worship Him
> who lives forever and ever…. (Revelation 4:8-10 NKJV)

There is also another portion of Scripture that tells us there are animals in heaven praising God —

> Then I looked, and I heard the voice of many angels
> around the throne, the **living creatures**, and the elders;
> and the number of them was ten thousand times ten thousand,
> and thousands of thousands, saying with a loud voice:

"Worthy is the Lamb who was slain to
receive power and riches and wisdom, and strength
and honor and glory and blessing!"

And *every creature* which is in heaven and on the
earth and under the earth and such as are in the sea,
and all that are in them, I heard *saying*:
"Blessing and honor and glory and power
Be to Him who sits on the throne,
And to the Lamb, forever and ever!"

Then the four living creatures **said,** "Amen!"
And the twenty-four elders fell down
And worshiped Him who lives forever and ever.
(Revelation 5:11-14 NKJV)

*When the Bible says every creature, it means **every** creature. Every creature includes the animals!*

When the Lamb opens the seals, it will be animals who declare, "Come and see." (Revelation 6:1, 3, 5, 7)

It is recorded in the Bible that animals have spoken here on earth.

Talking snake — Before the fall we have a talking serpent conversing with mankind. (See Genesis 3:1-5)

Talking donkey - Balaam's donkey speaks with words and rationally defends her actions. (See Numbers 22:28-30)

Talking bird —

Do not curse the king, even in your thought;
do not curse the rich, even in your bedroom;
For a *bird of the air may carry your voice,*
And a bird in flight may tell the matter.
(Ecclesiastes 10:20 NKJV)

The Psalmist tells us that the great sea creatures praise the Lord.

> Praise the Lord from the earth,
> You great sea creatures and all the depths;
> (Psalm 148:7 NKJV)

The very last words of the psalmist declares,

> "Let *everything* that has *breath* praise the Lord." (Psalm 150:6 NKJV)
> *Everything that has breath — includes the animals.*

> "… And *all flesh* shall bless His holy name forever and ever"
> (Psalm 145:21 NKJV)

> *All flesh includes the animals.*

Think about it, animals are found worshipping God throughout the Bible, both in heaven and on the earth. John said, "God is Spirit, and those who worship Him **must worship in spirit** and truth." (John 4:24 NKJV)

Animals would not be able to worship God if they were not spirit beings!

Animals understand the good news of the Gospel

When Jesus gave the great commission He said to them, "Go into all the world and preach the gospel to every *creature.*" (Mark 16:15 NKJV) Notice that He did not say preach the gospel to every *soul,* or to every *man* — He said preach the gospel to every *creature. Animals are creatures!*

This does not mean that the animals need to hear the gospel message for the purpose of being *born again* or to receive eternal security as is the case for mankind. *The spirits and souls of animals are already secure.* But what it *does* mean, is there's more to the message of the *gospel of the Kingdom of God, that Jesus preached.* The truth is, because animals have also been adversely affected by the fall, they too will benefit by hearing the good news that Jesus saves, heals, delivers and redeems. The Bible says in John 6:63 that the words of the gospel are *spirit and life. Certainly, animals understand the spirit on our spoken words!*

Animals will see the salvation of the Lord

The Book of Luke tells us, "..and *all flesh* shall see the salvation of God."
(Luke 3:6 NKJV)

Isaiah said;

"The glory of the Lord shall be revealed,
And *all flesh* shall see it together;
For the mouth of the Lord has spoken."
(Isaiah 40:5 NKJV)

The word *flesh* refers to both man and animals — *all flesh.*

All of creation, including the animals, will exalt the Lord

...that at the name of Jesus *every* knee should bow,
of those in heaven, and of those on earth,
and of those under the earth, and that *every* tongue
should confess that Jesus Christ is Lord,
to the glory of God the Father.
(Philippians 2:10-11 NKJV)

The earth, man, and the animals will be at peace after the judgments —
and Peace will reign forever on the New Earth.

The following passage from Isaiah paints a picture of what the earth will be like after the Lord returns and Satan is removed. There will be peace among the animals as they return to being herbivores, as they were originally created. That should be no surprise since that's the way it was before the fall, and that's the way it will be on the New Earth. There will be no killing — *not even for food.*

The present violence we experience worldwide today, is a direct result of the curse defined by God in the garden of Eden. This curse came as a result of *man's* sin. It is only because of Adam's fall that all of creation has had to suffer. But, on the New Earth — those of *us who love and care about the animals, will finally be in total* **ecstasy!**

> "The wolf also shall dwell with the lamb,
> The leopard shall lie down with the young goat,
> The calf and the young lion and the fatling together;
> And a little child shall lead them.
> The cow and the bear shall graze;
> Their young ones shall lie down together;
> And the lion shall eat straw like the ox.
> The nursing child shall play by the cobra's hole,
> And the weaned child shall put his hand in the viper's den.
> They shall not hurt nor destroy in all My holy mountain,
> For the earth shall be full of the knowledge of the Lord
> As the waters cover the sea." (Isaiah 11:6-9 NKJV)

The Spiritual Sensitivity of Animals

I have seen how animals respond to the presence of God, especially when people are praying or worshiping together. The animals often gather around wanting to be included. On the other hand, I have also observed how they bark or cringe when they perceive the presence of evil in the spirit realm.

It is my opinion, based on my own experience with animals, that animals are more intuitive and far more sensitive to the spirit realm than most people.

Our past, our present and our future — are in continuous relationship with the animals!

In reviewing the relationship between mankind and animals, there seems to be a pattern that runs throughout the Bible. When there's an announcement or a new beginning that takes place on the earth, man and animals are connected to one another.

It begins with the creation story, where Adam and Eve are in close relationship with the animals. (See Genesis 1:28)

Then, when the flood came, God saved the animals on the ark and included them in His covenant, along with Noah and his family. (See Genesis 7:7-9)

In the book of Exodus, Moses was tending his sheep when God called him to deliver His people out of the hand of the Egyptians. (See Exodus 3:1)

In the story of Jonah, the city of Nineva was granted a pardon because God cared not only for the people — but also for the animals. (See Jonah 4:11)

The birthplace of God's own Son was in a manger among the animals. (See Luke 2:7)

It was the shepherds and their sheep who first heard the good news of the birth of Jesus. (See Luke 2:8-13)

Immediately following His baptism, Jesus was taken into the wilderness where He was with the wild animals. (See Mark 1:12-13)

The Book of Hosea tells us that the suffering of animals is tied directly to man's sin. (See Hosea 4:1-3)

But then we learn in the book of Romans that the liberation of the animals from death and decay, is connected to man's redemption. (See Romans 8:19-21)

However, the most spectacular event of them all, will be the triumphant return of Jesus on none other than a magnificent white horse — *a symbol of righteousness and power.* Accompanying the Lord on His return will be the army of heaven — *all mounted on white horses.* (See Revelation 19:11-14)

*The Bible tells us from Genesis through Revelation, that man and animals have been in relationship since the beginning of creation. It also tells us, that the **redeemed** will live forever in relationship with the animals on the New Earth.*

ACCORDING TO THE BIBLE,
THE EARTH WILL NEVER BE WITHOUT ANIMALS

16

Tribute to—

Trinity Dancer

I remember a picture that hung on my bedroom wall when I was just a little girl. It was a profile picture of a beautiful, black legged bay filly. Whenever I would go into my room, it would *grab* my attention and *captivate* my heart. I had forgotten about that picture, until one day…

On Dancer's 30th birthday I said to the Lord, *"Thank you for blessing me with the most wonderful gift 30 years ago today. Little did I know on that early April morning what had been entrusted to my care — my dream, my assignment and the love of my life, all wrapped up in the most beautiful black legged, bay filly. What a treasure!"*

Dancer on her 30th Birthday

At that very moment, I recalled the picture from so many years ago. Simultaneously, I heard the Spirit of the Lord say to me, *"You saw her in your heart — long before you saw her with your eyes!"*

Don't ask me how, but I know it was my Dancer in the picture that hung on my wall so many years ago.

Trinity Dancer's name was divinely inspired

One day while I was putting on Dancer's fly mask, I whispered in her ear, "Jesus loves you, you're a gift from *heaven*." Then it hit me: *Dancer came from heaven above — through Heaven on earth.*

You see, Dancer's mother's name was Heaven — short for Heavenly Light.

Soon after I assisted Heaven with the birth of her first filly, I knew I had the privilege of giving her a name.

In the Thoroughbred industry, it's common to pick a name that includes something from the mother as well as something from the father. In horse breeding, lineage means a lot.

I remember praying to God about her name, *even though I didn't know Him.* I looked up the word 'heaven' and the word 'Trinity' came to my attention. There was something that resonated in my heart and I liked the sound of Trinity, so I looked it up to see what it meant. Even though its meaning didn't make much sense to me at the time — *I knew that was to be her name.*

Now the second half of her name, that was easy. After all, her grandfather is Northern Dancer! *And so, I named her — 'Trinity Dancer.'*

I had no idea the significance of my filly's name. That is, not until one day when I was talking with the Lord and He called her by name. But instead of saying Dancer as I call her, He called her 'Trinity.'

When I asked, *"Lord, why did you just call her 'Trinity?'"* He answered, *"Because, she represents Me!"*

And so, it's no surprise that Trinity Dancer also wears a white cross on her forehead. *After all, God knew that she would be on the cover of this book representing the eternal aspect of the animal kingdom.*

Suffice it to say, my relationship with Trinity Dancer has been supernatural!

Me and Trinity Dancer

I KNOW I'LL SPEND ETERNITY WITH MY PETS—

HOW ABOUT YOU?

Glossary

Adversary — Refers to Satan, *the devil.* He is our opponent and very real enemy.

Agape love — The selfless, sacrificial, unconditional, supernatural love of God. *Agape love is the most powerful force in the universe!*

Agrarian society — A community of individuals whose economy and wealth is primarily based on agriculture.

Angel of light — A term used to describe how Satan disguises himself to fool and deceive mankind. The Bible warns us that, "Satan himself masquerades as an angel of light." (2 Corinthians 11:14) *Be aware, Satan can disguise himself to make evil look good.*

Animal behaviorist — A person who studies the ways in which animals interact with each other, people, and the environment. They do this to determine what causes certain types of behavior and what factors can prompt behavior change — *especially as they occur in a natural environment.*

Animal rights — The right of an animal to be protected from exploitation and abuse by humans.

Animal rights activist — Someone who is concerned about the welfare and treatment of animals and takes a stand against the cruelty and exploitation that causes them harm.

Animal vivisection — Cutting into or performing operations on live animals.

Annihilate — To completely destroy someone or something to where it ceases to exist — *obliteration.*

Anointing — The power of the Holy Spirit working in and through the life of a believer to accomplish the will of God.

Antichrist — Man of sin, son of perdition. An opponent or adversary of the Messiah. The Antichrist is an individual possessed by Satan. He will rise up in the last days to rule the world and oppose Christ and His followers. Along with the help of the False Prophet, he will usher in the worst and most troubled times the world has or ever will experience —a time of *great tribulation.*

But ultimately, the Antichrist and the False Prophet will both be thrown into the lake of fire!

Armor of God — Spiritual elements that are essential for every believer to wear in order to fight and win every spiritual battle. (Ephesians 6:12-17)

Asperger syndrome — A developmental disorder related to autism. It is characterized by higher than average intellectual ability coupled with impaired social skills, and restrictive, repetitive patterns of interest and activities.

Attributes — A quality or feature regarded as a characteristic or inherent part of an animal or person.

Authority — The legal or rightful power that is exercised by a person who has been given dominion over something or someone.

Autism — A condition that is present from early childhood and characterized by a difficulty in communicating and forming relationships with other people, and in using language and abstract concepts.

Autism spectrum disorder — A spectrum of closely related disorders with a shared core of symptoms that impair a person's ability to communicate and interact with others.

B

Beast — Refers to an animal. However, there is one exception in the Book of Revelation where the word "beast" is referring to the "anti-christ."

Benefit — An advantage or profit gained from something.

Benevolent — Demeanor characterized by the expression of kind feelings, compassion and charity. Benevolence is established for doing righteous works. The word benevolent comes from two Latin words: *bene* which means "well" and *volent* that means "to wish" — *to wish well.*

Blessing — An empowerment bestowed to prosper, to succeed, to multiply, to increase, and to excel. The very first words God spoke over creation was *the blessing.* (See Genesis 1:28)

Bondage of corruption — A state of being bound by and subjected to moral perversion and depravity.

Born again — Literally means *born from above.* To undergo a spiritual rebirth or a regeneration of the human spirit by the Holy Spirit — *a new birth.* Those who are born again have become a *child of God.*

Breath of life — The spiritual breath of God that brings life into a created being.

By-product — A secondary or incidental product; the result of another action.

C

Cast out — To be forcefully removed from the presence of a loving God. To drive out, expel, send away. No one has to be cast out. Jesus said..., "...I will most certainly not cast out [I will never, no never, reject one of them who comes to Me]." (John 6:37 AMPC)

Chaos — A condition or state of complete and utter disorder and confusion.

Characteristic — A distinctive quality or feature of an animal that distinguishes them.

Child of God — Someone who is *born again* and spiritually renewed. In other words, someone adopted by God as His child.

Children of God — Those who have put their faith in Jesus Christ — *are the children of God.*

Christ — This is *not* Jesus' last name, but rather it literally means "The Anointed One."

Christian — A born again believer who is truly a disciple of Jesus Christ — in other words, *a follower of Christ.* A Christian is someone who has put their faith and trust in Jesus Christ and the finished work He did on the cross at Calvary; that is, His death, burial and resurrection. *A Christian is a child of God.*

Christianity — *Is more than just a religion* — it is a way of life based on a person's love for God and love for people. The key difference that separates Christianity from other belief systems is — Christians have a covenant relationship with a living God through His Son, Jesus Christ.

Cohort — Any group of soldiers or warriors.

Colossal — Something extraordinarily great in size, extent, or degree — *gigantic.*

Communion — To be in intimate fellowship with God. Also a ceremony involving bread and drink to commemorate what Jesus did on the cross.

Complex automata — A false opinion about animals that says: they are complex but they function automatically or instinctively — *without any reasoning ability!*

Condemn — To pronounce to be guilty and sentence to severe punishment for sinning — *judge to be wrong.*

Condemned — Someone pronounced guilty and sentenced to severe punishment.

Covenant — A conditional promise made to man and creation by God, as revealed in Scripture. From a biblical perspective, a covenant implies much more than a contract or agreement between two parties.

Covenant people —Those who are in covenant relationship with God.

Covenant promise — A promise made by God to both man and creation — *this includes the animals.*

Creator — The One who created the world and all that is in it — God.

Creature — A living, breathing being who has a soul. The Hebrew word for creature is "nephesh" — meaning *soul.* Both man and animals are creatures.

Cross — *The cross is not referring to a wooden beam or a piece of jewelry.* The cross refers to all that Jesus accomplished at Calvary through His death, burial and resurrection. The message of the cross of Jesus Christ is that He saves, delivers and heals. This is the single most important message of the Word of God, as well as the most controversial in world history! (see 1 Corinthians 1:18)

Curse — A solemn utterance intended to invoke a supernatural power to inflict harm or punishment on someone or something. When made by God it has prophetic value and force. A curse is what we get when we disdain or scorn God's blessing. *We can choose to live under the curse or under the blessing.* (Deuteronomy 30:19 NKJV)

D

Death — A form of separation and is commonly recognized when the spirit and soul depart from the physical body — *referred to as physical death.*

But death can also refer to spiritual death — *spiritual separation from God.* Death does **NOT** mean non-existence. (See Genesis 2:17 Also, see definition for Spiritual death.)

Deceive — To mislead by a false appearance or statement —to cause someone to believe a lie.

Deception — Something that deceives or is intended to deceive; or causes someone to accept as true what is false.

Degradation — To bring into a state of demoralization.

Deliverance — The act of being rescued or set free from bondage — *as in salvation.*

Demilitarized zone — A specified area where military use is forbidden, or excluded — considered neutral territory. Satan does not fight fair. *There is no area where he withholds his military forces from attacking.* Only the blood of Jesus Christ can put you in a safe zone!

Depravity — An established condition of moral corruption and perversion where there is a total lack of morals, values, and even regard for other living things.

Desolate — A lonely deserted place that's in a state of bleak and dismal emptiness.

Despair — Total loss of hope and expectation, usually accompanied by apathy and low spirits.

Destiny — The ultimate fate or future for both man and animal.

Destroyed — Cease to be — *annihilated.*

Detriment — Harm causing loss, damage, disadvantage, or injury on a personal level.

Devil — The supreme spirit of evil; an inferior and evil spirit at enmity with God. The devil is a fallen archangel who was expelled from heaven for rebelling against God. *There is only one devil but many demons. He is the implacable archenemy and tempter of the entire human race.* In the Greek his name is Satan, which means "the false accuser" or "the slanderer." In the Hebrew his name means "adversary."

Divine — Relating to God the Supreme Being.

Divine Intervention — When God gets involved in your life. It can be God causing something to happen, or God preventing something from happening.

Divine Providence — The foreseeing care and guidance of God over the creatures of the earth. It includes the intentional and strategic positioning of animals among mankind in a state of coexistence.

Doctrine — A system of beliefs and teachings. For the Christian faith, doctrines are based on the unchanging Word of God — *the Bible.*

Dominion — The authority and power to govern and control.

Dominion should be expressed as service — a sacrificial contribution that serves God and the common good. Dominion was not given to man for the purpose of dominating over other people.

Dumb donkey — Refers to a donkey who lacks the capability of using human speech. *Dumb* does not mean a lack of intelligence, good judgment, stupidity or dull-witted. Author: *Simply speech-impaired.*

E

Ecstasy — Excessive joy; rapture, extreme delight; delightful beyond measure. *This is not referring to the illegal drug,"MDMA."* Such drugs are merely the devil's cheap counterfeits that are intended to lead to destruction.

Egotistical — Excessively conceited or absorbed in oneself; indifferent to the well-being of others — *self-centered.*

El Shaddai — A name of God Almighty — specifically, the All-Sufficient One — All mighty, All powerful, Omnipotent!

Empathize — The ability to identify and understand the feelings and thoughts of another. To relate to the emotional experience of either another person or an animal.

Enigma — A mystery; a quandary.

Eternal damnation — The state of being condemned to eternal punishment in the *Lake of Fire.*

Eternal death — Unending separation from God, as well as all animals and people in a place called the lake of fire. It is the *third type* of death in the Bible, and also is referred to as the *second death.* This is the ultimate form of separation — eternal death is irreversible!

Eternal destiny — A future without end.

Eternal life — Is everlasting, never ending life. Eternal life is knowing God. This refers to having an intimate, close, personal relationship with God. The gift of eternal life comes to those who believe in Jesus Christ, who is Himself "the resurrection and the life…" (See John 11:25)

Eternal spirit being — The immortal part of both man and animals that will continue to exist forever.

Eternity —A duration or continuance without beginning or end. For the purpose of this book, *eternity* is referring to an endless period of time after death. *Only God has existed from eternity.*

Everlasting covenant — A perpetual covenant that is a promise between God and man. The Bible is a covenant document and only God can make an everlasting covenant. The Old and New Testaments are in fact, Old and New Covenants. This is how God deals with man and His creation — *through His covenants.*

Evil — Wicked, corrupt, depraved; corruption of the heart. The force or spirit in this world system that governs and gives rise to wickedness and sin — *that is Satan.*

Evolved — Developed gradually from a simple form to a more complex form.

Exploitation — The abusive use of someone or something for one's own gain or advantage — *selfish utilization, as in the exploitation of animals.*

F

Fallen angels — Angels who rebelled against God and were cast out of heaven. They are eternal, supernatural, wicked spirit beings. Their destiny will be forever in the eternal fire. (Matthew 25:41)

Fiery darts — Satan's thoughts and suggestions that are sent like missiles or arrows into our minds to attempt to deceive us, in order to aid him in advancing his kingdom of darkness. (Ephesians 6:16 NKJV)

Finished work of the cross — All that Jesus accomplished through His death, burial and resurrection — *including the redemption of all of creation*. It was at the cross, where the judgment of God against our sin was endured by Christ, who became our substitute in order to become our Savior. *Jesus paid it all at the cross!*

Fruit of the Spirit — The spiritual attitudes that are present in a person's life when they follow God's Holy Spirit: love, joy, peace, long-suffering, kindness, goodness, faithfulness, gentleness, and self-control. (See Galatians 5:22, 23)

G

Glorified body — Refers to a resurrected physical body that has been perfected and set free from the effects of sin. It's a body that's incorruptible and immortal — *bringing glory to God.*

Glorify — To acknowledge God for His greatness — to magnify and make Him large. We glorify God when we honor, praise, worship and reverence Him. We glorify God when we let His presence be known.

Glory — Used to speak of great honor, praise, value, wonder, and splendor. In the Hebrew it means *weight* or *heaviness. The Glory is the manifested presence of God.*

god of this world — Refers to Satan and the influence that he has on the ideas, opinions, goals, hopes and views of the majority of people. He is also called the "prince of the power of the air." (Ephesians 2:2)

These titles denote Satan's capabilities. But this does not mean that he rules the world completely or that he has ultimate authority. *The truth is, believers are no longer under the rule of Satan* (See Colossians 1:13). *However, he does rule over the unbelieving world in a very specific way. 2 Corinthians 4:4 reveals what Satan has done to get unbelievers to follow his agenda:* "**The god of this world** *has blinded the minds of unbelievers, so that they cannot see the light of the gospel of the glory of Christ.*"

God's plan of redemption — The plan that purchased back all that was lost in the *fall of man* through the shed blood of the sacrifice of God's own Son —*Jesus Christ.*

Gospel — The good news of what Jesus accomplished for mankind and creation; revealed in God's written word — the Holy Bible.

Gospel of the kingdom — The good news message of repentance, redemption, and restoration that is offered by God to all who will receive Jesus Christ. Those who accept Jesus as their Lord and Savior become part of His eternal kingdom.

Great White Throne Judgment — Final judgment prior to the lost being cast into the lake of fire. (See Revelation 20:11-15). Those who are lost (unregenerate man) and without hope, will still be resurrected and stand before the great white throne for judgment.

Heaven — A real place as described in the Bible.

Hell — A temporary place where the souls of the unrighteous are kept as they await the final resurrection — *that is, all who have rejected Jesus Christ.* At that time, they will stand before God for the Great White

Throne Judgment and receive their final sentence of eternal punishment, in the *lake of fire.* (See Revelation 20:1-15)

High treason — Referring to the violation of allegiance to the will and word of God that Adam committed in the garden of Eden.

His word — The Bible; a document that is alive with the Spirit of God. *His word* is more than printed words on a page — *it is God speaking to the human race!*

Holy — The term holy is applied to persons or objects that have some type of relationship with the Lord, meaning — *they are set apart for His service.*

Holy Spirit — Since God is spirit, this is why the Third Person of the Trinity is called the Holy Spirit. He too is fully God, and all three Persons of the Trinity are holy and have the weight of glory abounding in them.

Hope — The *modern* idea of hope is "to wish for, to expect, but without certainty of the fulfillment; to desire but with no real assurance of getting your desire." *Biblical* hope on the other hand, is an indication of certainty. "Hope" in Scripture means "a strong and confident expectation." *Hope is comparable to trust and a confident expectation.*

I

Ignorant — is *not knowing.* It means to lack essential knowledge, information or awareness.

Incorruptible — Not subject to death or decay; an everlasting condition or state.

Indestructible — Unable to be destroyed.

Innate — Something that exists at the time of birth; inborn, inherent.

Innocent — Free from moral wrong; without sin — pure.

Instinct — A natural ability that helps you decide what to do or how to act without thinking.

Intangible — Not having physical presence; incapable of being perceived by the senses.

Intelligence — The capacity for learning, reasoning, and understanding; aptitude in grasping truths, relationships, facts, meanings, etc. Intelligence is also defined as mental alertness or quickness of understanding.

K

Kainos (Greek origin) — Something that is newly restored to a condition that is better than its original condition.

Karma — A false belief supporting reincarnation. This belief says the sum of a person's actions in this state and previous states of existence, determines their fate in a future existence.

Knowledge — Acquaintance with facts, truths, or principles.

Kosmos (Greek origin) — The entire created world order.

L

Lake of Fire — The *final destination* for those who reject Jesus Christ. It follows the Great White Throne Judgment and is also known as the *second death*. It is described as a place of burning sulfur. Those in it experience eternal, unspeakable torment of an unrelenting nature. The lake of fire is the place of eternal punishment for all unrepentant sinners

— truly, *it's a lake that burns forever and ever!* (See Mark 9:45-46; Revelation 19:20; 20:10, 14-15; 21:8)

Life — A living soul. (as referenced in this book.)

Living creature — A soul; refers to both man and animal. Translated from the Hebrew word *nephesh*.

Lord — The meaning of *Lord* is much more than a title of honor or respect. To say Jesus is Lord is declaring His deity — *it means that Jesus is God.* When you declare Him as your Lord, you are saying that you commit yourself to His Lordship — to obey Him: to submit to the authority of His word and Spirit. If Jesus is your Lord, then He owns you and has the right to tell you what to do. Anyone who says, "Jesus is Lord," with a full understanding of the meaning has been divinely enlightened. 1 Corinthians 12:3 says, "No one can say, 'Jesus is Lord,' except by the Holy Spirit."

M

Mankind — Refers to human beings collectively; the human race.

Messiah — Refers to the promised deliverer of the Jewish nation.

Minions — The fallen angels or underlings who follow and serve Satan.

Monger — Refers to a person who is involved with something in a petty or contemptible way.

Mortal body — A physical body subject to death; having a transitory life in this world as apposed to a spiritual body that is eternal.

N

Narcissistic — Having an inordinate fascination with oneself; excessive self-love and vanity.

Natural realm — An understanding of life based on sense knowledge. This is in contrast to the *spirit realm* which supersedes and is greater than the natural realm.

Neo (Greek origin) — Refers to something that is new in relationship to time.

New Covenant — Is based on what Jesus Christ accomplished on the cross. Covenant people are God's people — *the redeemed.* They have a promise from God for eternal salvation. This is true for anyone who has put their faith in Jesus Christ and the finished work on the cross at Calvary. Covenant people are entitled to everything that was purchased by Jesus Christ on the cross.

O

Old Covenant — The complete Bible of the Jews. It consists of the Law, the Prophets and the Hagiographa, being the first of the two main divisions of the Christian Bible. It encompasses the original agreement God made with mankind that includes His commands.

Ominous — Giving the impression that something bad or unpleasant is going to happen; threatening; inauspicious.

Omnipotent — Comes from *omni* meaning "all" and *potent* meaning "power." God is omnipotent because He has all power over all things.

Only Begotten Son — Refers to the one and only Son of God, born supernaturally in fulfillment of biblical prophecy — *Jesus Christ, the Savior of the world.* (See 1 John 4:14; John 3;16)

Open his eyes — The act of having spiritual eyes opened to observe spiritual realm insights.

Overcome — To live by faith in Jesus Christ as your Lord and Savior.

P

Pandora's box — A prolific source of unforeseen and extensive troubles or problems.

Passing — Refers to the death or departure of a person or an animal.

Perception — An awareness of the environment through the physical senses.

Philosophy — A particular set of beliefs and principles.

Physical death — When the spirit and soul depart from the body.

Pie in the Sky — A phrase that means an empty wish or promise.

Predetermined — Established or decided in advance.

Preeminence — A state or character of being above or before others; superior; outstanding.

Preserve — To rescue, save and bring victory. *To keep alive or in existence – to make everlasting.*

Purgatory — Believed by some, to be a place where a Christian's soul goes after death to be cleansed of the sins that had not been fully satisfied during this life. What does the Bible say about purgatory? *The Bible says nothing about Purgatory!* The doctrine of purgatory is not a Scriptural concept. There is however, much discussion in God's word about the only two destinations for those who have died: heaven and hell!

R

Random chance — Lacking any definite plan or prearranged order; haphazard. *It is impossible for random chance to occur in the created order.*

Reconcile — Means to be made "at one" with God — having fellowship and peace with God where once there was enmity. Reconciliation is atonement (at-one-ment).

Redeem — To purchase back, to ransom, to liberate or rescue from captivity or bondage — *to recover.*

Redeemed — The past tense of the word redeem. It means to be rescued and delivered from the bondage of sin and the penalties of God's violated law. It's what Jesus Christ did for us when He gave His life.

Reincarnation — A spiritual deception that is based on the law of karma that says the physical life you live now is the result of your past physical lives, and that your future lives depend on karma.

Religion — For the purpose of this book, religion is referring to man's vain attempt to reach God through a set of beliefs, ceremonies and rituals. Religion is about what man must DO to be right with God. Christianity is about what God has already DONE to reach man.

Repugnant — Repulsive, revolting, detestable, abominable and vile.

Restored — The biblical meaning for *restored* is to receive more back than what was lost. The final state is always greater than the original condition with God.

Resurrection — When the physical body is raised up from the grave. The bodies of the righteous will be restored to a glorified condition, while the bodies of the wicked will be resurrected to stand before the Great White Throne Judgment. *The bodies of the animals will also be resurrected— raised up along with the righteous, to an everlasting glorified condition. But they will not stand in judgment before God.*

Reunion — When two or more come together after a period of separation.

Revelation — A disclosing or uncovering of something previously hidden. Revelation is knowledge from God to man that would otherwise not be known.

Righteousness — Means you are in right standing with God. Righteousness cannot be attained by man on his own — *the standard is too high*. True righteousness can only be possible through the shed blood of Jesus Christ because His blood is the only thing that has the power to cleanse us from all sin. *The Bible tells us that born again believers possess the righteousness of Christ; "For our sake he made him to be sin who knew no sin, so that in him we might become the righteousness of God."* (2 Corinthians 5:21 ESV)

S

Sacrifice — To give up something valuable for the sake of another. To make atonement for sin. For something to be a sacrifice it must have great value and meet certain qualifications. *It was a sacrifice for God when He gave His only begotten Son, Jesus Christ, to atone for the sins of mankind!*

Salvation — The deliverance from the power of sin and it's consequences. We receive salvation by having faith in Jesus Christ and the finished work of the cross at Calvary. *Salvation is the act of being rescued or saved from the punishment of sin.* Salvation for the animals is the deliverance from the effects of man's sin.

Satan — Is a fallen angelic creature who will end up for all of eternity in the lake of fire. (Revelation 20:10) In the Greek, Satan means *false accuser or slanderer*. In the Hebrew, Satan means *adversary*. (See definition for Devil)

Saved — To be born again from above; to be made spiritually alive or renewed.

Savior — Is One who delivers, preserves and rescues. To those who are redeemed, Jesus Christ is their Savior.

Scripture — The sacred writings of both the Old and New Testaments. Scripture can also refer to a particular passage from the Bible.

Second birth — To be *born again,* which literally means *born from above.* The second birth is a spiritual birth and is essential for one to go to heaven. (See John 3:3)

Second death — An everlasting eternal death and separation from God. The second death is synonymous with the *lake of fire.*

Selah — Means to pause and meditate on what you have just read.

Sin — To violate the revealed will of God's holy standard of righteousness; to miss the mark — *as in archery.*

Sleep — The biblical term for physical death.

Soul — Made up of the mind, the will, and the emotions. The soul is intangible and immortal.

Sovereign — The ultimate source of authority and power of God. It means He is Almighty God and the Most High God.

Spirit — When capitalized, it is referring to the Holy Spirit of God.

spirit — From the Hebrew word "ruwach" which means *breath.*

Spirit realm — An immaterial, unseen spiritual reality. The spirit realm consists of both good and evil. Even though the spirit realm is invisible to the physical eye, we are connected to it, and what goes on in the spirit realm directly affects our physical world. The spirit realm is eternal as apposed to temporal. *The spirit realm is the supernatural realm.*

Spiritual death — The condition of man's spirit when he is disconnected from his life source — God. Be aware, when you are separated from God — *you are connected to Satan.* Unless spiritual death is reversed in this life, the result will be eternal death.

Spiritually alive — To be reconnected to the source of all life — God. In other words, it means to have been *born again.*

Spiritually dead — Someone who has not been *born again.*

Stewardship — When someone manages the possessions of another. For example: God has entrusted the animals to our care and one day we will each have to give an account for how we have managed what has been given to us. *God alone has full rights of ownership.*

Supernatural insight — Insight above and beyond what is natural or explainable by natural laws.

Supernatural realm — See above definition for *spirit realm.*

T

Tapestry of eternity — An intricate or complex combination of things woven together to produce a design — *as in God's creation.* The characteristics and attributes of animals are significant and integral threads in this tapestry.

The fall of man — The precipitous decline of human beings into a state of natural or innate sinfulness through the sin of Adam when he rebelled against a loving God.

Transcends — To be or go beyond the range or limit of time and space.

Tree of the Knowledge of Good and Evil — An actual tree that existed in the midst of the garden of Eden. In disobedience, Adam and Eve ate of the fruit of this tree against the command of God. This was the first sin committed by man. (See Genesis 2:9; 3:1-7)

Trinity — A word used to express the doctrine of the union of three distinct eternal Persons in one Godhead — the Father is God, the Son is God, and the Holy Spirit is God.

U

Unadulterated truth — Pure and untainted truth.

Unregenerate man — A person who is at enmity with God — *a lost soul.*

Utopian — Idealistic and unrealistic.

V

Vapor — A fleeting moment in time. Life is short and uncertain and there are no guarantees about tomorrow. (See James 4:14)

Veil — Something that covers, separates, screens or conceals.

Vision — To see a picture-like message in the spirit realm.

W

Welfare — Refers to the well-being, safety, protection, prosperity, good fortune, and best interest of the recipient.

World system — A term that comes from the Greek word kosmos. It is not referring to the physical planet but rather to society, human culture, social order, and the culture of the nations. The *world system* involves a concern for external appearances more than inner content and quality and is actually mankind and society functioning without God. *The world system, is a system that opposes the Word of God and is governed by Satan!*

Wrath of God — Is holy and always justified, yet a fearsome and terrifying thing. The wrath of God will be poured out in the last days and it will be an intense season of fear for those who don't want a relationship with the God of love. (See Revelation 6:14-17) God's wrath is to be feared because God promises eternal punishment apart from Christ. (Matthew 25:46)

Made in the USA
Columbia, SC
06 August 2020

15703056R00124